CLEP-17 COLLEGE-LEVEL EXAMINATION
PROGRAM SERIES

*This is your
PASSBOOK for...*

Human Growth and Development

*Test Preparation Study Guide
Questions & Answers*

NATIONAL LEARNING CORPORATION®

COPYRIGHT NOTICE

This book is SOLELY intended for, is sold ONLY to, and its use is RESTRICTED to individual, bona fide applicants or candidates who qualify by virtue of having seriously filed applications for appropriate license, certificate, professional and/or promotional advancement, higher school matriculation, scholarship, or other legitimate requirements of education and/or governmental authorities.

This book is NOT intended for use, class instruction, tutoring, training, duplication, copying, reprinting, excerption, or adaptation, etc., by:

1) Other publishers
2) Proprietors and/or Instructors of "Coaching" and/or Preparatory Courses
3) Personnel and/or Training Divisions of commercial, industrial, and governmental organizations
4) Schools, colleges, or universities and/or their departments and staffs, including teachers and other personnel
5) Testing Agencies or Bureaus
6) Study groups which seek by the purchase of a single volume to copy and/or duplicate and/or adapt this material for use by the group as a whole without having purchased individual volumes for each of the members of the group
7) Et al.

Such persons would be in violation of appropriate Federal and State statutes.

PROVISION OF LICENSING AGREEMENTS – Recognized educational, commercial, industrial, and governmental institutions and organizations, and others legitimately engaged in educational pursuits, including training, testing, and measurement activities, may address request for a licensing agreement to the copyright owners, who will determine whether, and under what conditions, including fees and charges, the materials in this book may be used them. In other words, a licensing facility exists for the legitimate use of the material in this book on other than an individual basis. However, it is asseverated and affirmed here that the material in this book CANNOT be used without the receipt of the express permission of such a licensing agreement from the Publishers. Inquiries re licensing should be addressed to the company, attention rights and permissions department.

All rights reserved, including the right of reproduction in whole or in part, in any form or by any means, electronic or mechanical, including photocopying, recording, or by any information storage and retrieval system, without permission in writing from the Publisher.

Copyright © 2025 by
National Learning Corporation

212 Michael Drive, Syosset, NY 11791
(516) 921-8888 • www.passbooks.com
E-mail: info@passbooks.com

PASSBOOK® SERIES

THE *PASSBOOK® SERIES* has been created to prepare applicants and candidates for the ultimate academic battlefield – the examination room.

At some time in our lives, each and every one of us may be required to take an examination – for validation, matriculation, admission, qualification, registration, certification, or licensure.

Based on the assumption that every applicant or candidate has met the basic formal educational standards, has taken the required number of courses, and read the necessary texts, the *PASSBOOK® SERIES* furnishes the one special preparation which may assure passing with confidence, instead of failing with insecurity. Examination questions – together with answers – are furnished as the basic vehicle for study so that the mysteries of the examination and its compounding difficulties may be eliminated or diminished by a sure method.

This book is meant to help you pass your examination provided that you qualify and are serious in your objective.

The entire field is reviewed through the huge store of content information which is succinctly presented through a provocative and challenging approach – the question-and-answer method.

A climate of success is established by furnishing the correct answers at the end of each test.

You soon learn to recognize types of questions, forms of questions, and patterns of questioning. You may even begin to anticipate expected outcomes.

You perceive that many questions are repeated or adapted so that you can gain acute insights, which may enable you to score many sure points.

You learn how to confront new questions, or types of questions, and to attack them confidently and work out the correct answers.

You note objectives and emphases, and recognize pitfalls and dangers, so that you may make positive educational adjustments.

Moreover, you are kept fully informed in relation to new concepts, methods, practices, and directions in the field.

You discover that you are actually taking the examination all the time: you are preparing for the examination by "taking" an examination, not by reading extraneous and/or supererogatory textbooks.

In short, this PASSBOOK®, used directedly, should be an important factor in helping you to pass your test.

NONTRADITIONAL EDUCATION

Students returning to school as adults bring more varied experience to their studies than do the teenagers who begin college shortly after graduating from high school. As a result, there are numerous programs for students with nontraditional learning curves. Hundreds of colleges and universities grant degrees to people who cannot attend classes at a regular campus or have already learned what the college is supposed to teach.

You can earn nontraditional education credits in many ways:
- Passing standardized exams
- Demonstrating knowledge gained through experience
- Completing campus-based coursework, and
- Taking courses off campus

Some methods of assessing learning for credit are objective, such as standardized tests. Others are more subjective, such as a review of life experiences.

With some help from four hypothetical characters – Alice, Vin, Lynette, and Jorge – this article describes nontraditional ways of earning educational credit. It begins by describing programs in which you can earn a high school diploma without spending 4 years in a classroom. The college picture is more complicated, so it is presented in two parts: one on gaining credit for what you know through course work or experience, and a second on college degree programs. The final section lists resources for locating more information.

Earning High School Credit

People who were prevented from finishing high school as teenagers have several options if they want to do so as adults. Some major cities have back-to-school programs that allow adults to attend high school classes with current students. But the more practical alternatives for most adults are to take the General Educational Development (GED) tests or to earn a high school diploma by demonstrating their skills or taking correspondence classes.

Of course, these options do not match the experience of staying in high school and graduating with one's friends. But they are viable alternatives for adult learners committed to meeting and, often, continuing their educational goals.

GED Program

Alice quit high school her sophomore year and took a job to help support herself, her younger brother, and their newly widowed mother. Now an adult, she wants to earn her high school diploma – and then go on to college. Because her job as head cook and her family responsibilities keep her busy during the day, she plans to get a high school equivalency diploma. She will study for, and take, the GED tests. Every year, about half a million adults earn their high school credentials this way. A GED diploma is accepted in lieu of a high school one by more than 90 percent of employers, colleges, and universities, so it is a good choice for someone like Alice.

The GED testing program is sponsored by the American Council on Education and State and local education departments. It consists of examinations in five subject areas: Writing, science, mathematics, social studies, and literature and the arts. The tests also measure skills such as analytical ability, problem solving, reading comprehension, and ability to understand and apply information. Most of the questions are multiple choice; the writing test includes an essay section on a topic of general interest.

Eligibility rules for taking the exams vary, but some states require that you must be at least 18. Tests are given in English, Spanish, and French. In addition to standard print, versions in large print, Braille, and audiocassette are also available. Total time allotted for the tests is 7 1/2 hours.

The GED tests are not easy. About one-fourth of those who complete the exams every year do not pass. Passing scores are established by administering the tests to a sample of graduating high school seniors. The minimum standard score is set so that about one-third of graduating seniors would not pass the tests if they took them.

Because of the difficulty of the tests, people need to prepare themselves to take them. Often, they start by taking the Official GED Practice Tests, usually available through a local adult education center. Centers are listed in your phone book's blue pages under "Adult Education," "Continuing Education," or "GED." Adult education centers also have information about GED preparation classes and self-study materials. Classes are generally arranged to accommodate adults' work schedules. National Learning Corporation publishes several study guides that aim to thoroughly prepare test-takers for the GED.

School districts, colleges, adult education centers, and community organizations have information about GED testing schedules and practice tests. For more information, contact them, your nearest GED testing center, or:

GED Testing Service
One Dupont Circle, NW, Suite 250
Washington, DC 20036-1163
1(800) 62-MY GED (626-9433)
(202) 939-9490

Skills Demonstration

Adults who have acquired high school level skills through experience might be eligible for the National External Diploma Program. This alternative to the GED does not involve any direct instruction. Instead, adults seeking a high school diploma must demonstrate mastery of 65 competencies in 8 general areas: Communication; computation; occupational preparedness; and self, social, consumer, scientific, and technological awareness.

Mastery is shown through the completion of the tasks. For example, a participant could prove competency in computation by measuring a room for carpeting, figuring out the amount of carpet needed, and computing the cost.

Before being accepted for the program, adults undergo an evaluation. Tests taken at one of the program's offices measure reading, writing, and mathematics abilities. A take-home segment includes a self-assessment of current skills, an individual skill evaluation, and an occupational interest and aptitude test.

Adults accepted for the program have weekly meetings with an assessor. At the meeting, the assessor reviews the participant's work from the previous week. If the task has not been completed properly, the assessor explains the mistake. Participants continue to correct their errors until they master each competency. A high school diploma is awarded upon proven mastery of all 65 competencies.

Fourteen States and the District of Columbia now offer the External Diploma Program. For more information, contact:

External Diploma Program
One Dupont Circle, NW, Suite 250
Washington, DC 20036-1193
(202) 939-9475

Correspondence and Distance Study

Vin dropped out of high school during his junior year because his family's frequent moves made it difficult for him to continue his studies. He promised himself at the time he dropped out that he would someday finish the courses needed for his diploma. For people like Vin, who prefer to earn a traditional diploma in a nontraditional way, there are about a dozen accredited courses of study for earning a high school diploma by correspondence, or distance study. The programs are either privately run, affiliated with a university, or administered by a State education department.

Distance study diploma programs have no residency requirements, allowing students to continue their studies from almost any location. Depending on the course of study, students need not be enrolled full time and usually have more flexible schedules for finishing their work. Selection of courses ranges from vo-tech to college prep, and some programs place different emphasis on the types of diplomas offered. University affiliated schools, for example, allow qualified students to take college courses along with their high school ones. Students can then apply the college credits toward a degree at that university or transfer them to another institution.

Taking courses by distance study is often more challenging and time consuming than attending classes, especially for adults who have other obligations. Success depends on each student's motivation. Students usually do reading assignments on their own. Written exercises, which they complete and send to an instructor for grading, supplement their reading material.

A list of some accredited high schools that offer diplomas by distance study is available free from the Distance Education and Training Council, formerly known as the National Home Study Council. Request the "DETC Directory of Accredited Institutions" from:

The Distance Education and Training Council
1601 18th Street, NW.
Washington, DC 20009-2529
(202) 234-5100

Some publications profiling nontraditional college programs include addresses and descriptions of several high school correspondence ones. See the Resources section at the end of this article for more information.

Getting College Credit For What You Know

Adults can receive college credit for prior coursework, by passing examinations, and documenting experiential learning. With help from a college advisor, nontraditional students should assess their skills, establish their educational goals, and determine the number of college credits they might be eligible for.

Even before you meet with a college advisor, you should collect all your school and training records. Then, make a list of all knowledge and abilities acquired through experience, no matter how irrelevant they seem to your chosen field. Next, determine your educational goals: What specific field do you wish to study? What kind of a degree do you want? Finally, determine how your past work fits into the field of study. Later on, you will evaluate educational programs to find one that's right for you.

People who have complex educational or experiential learning histories might want to have their learning evaluated by the Regents Credit Bank. The Credit Bank, operated by Regents College of the University of the State of New York, allows people to consolidate credits earned through college, experience, or other methods. Special assessments are available for Regents College enrollees whose knowledge in a specific field cannot be adequately evaluated by standardized exams. For more information, contact the Regents Credit Bank at:

Regents College
7 Columbia Circle
Albany, NY 12203-5159
(518) 464-8500

Credit For Prior College Coursework

When Lynette was in college during the 1970s, she attended several different schools and took a variety of courses. She did well in some classes and poorly in others. Now that she is a successful business owner and has more focus, Lynette thinks she should forget about her previous coursework and start from scratch. Instead, she should start from where she is.

Lynette should have all her transcripts sent to the colleges or universities of her choice and let an admissions officer determine which classes are applicable toward a degree. A few credits here and there may not seem like much, but they add up. Even if the subjects do not seem relevant to any major, they might be counted as elective credits toward a degree. And comparing the cost of transcripts with the cost of college courses, it makes sense to spend a few dollars per transcript for a chance to save hundreds, and perhaps thousands, of dollars in books and tuition.

Rules for transferring credits apply to all prior coursework at accredited colleges and universities, whether done on campus or off. Courses completed off campus, often called extended learning, include those available to students through independent study and correspondence. Many schools have extended learning programs; Brigham Young University, for example, offers more than 300 courses through its Department of Independent Study. One type of extended learning is distance learning, a form of correspondence study by technological means such as television, video and audio, CD-ROM, electronic mail, and computer tutorials. See the Resources section at the end of this article for more information about publications available from the National University Continuing Education Association.

Any previously earned college credits should be considered for transfer, no matter what the subject or the grade received. Many schools do not accept the transfer of courses graded below a C or ones taken more than a designated number of years ago. Some colleges and universities also have limits on the number of credits that can be transferred and applied toward a degree. But not all do. For example, Thomas Edison State College, New Jersey's State college for adults, accepts the transfer of all 120 hours of credit required for a baccalaureate degree – provided all the credits are transferred from regionally accredited schools, no more than 80 are at the junior college level, and the student's grades overall and in the field of study average out to C.

To assign credit for prior coursework, most schools require original transcripts. This means you must complete a form or send a written, signed request to have your transcripts released directly to a college or university. Once you have chosen the schools you want to apply to, contact the schools you attended before. Find out how much each transcript costs, and ask them to send your transcripts to the ones you are applying to. Write a letter that includes your name (and names used during attendance, if different) and dates of attendance, along with the names and addresses of the schools to which your transcripts should be sent. Include payment and mail to the registrar at the schools you have attended. The registrar's office will process your request and send an official transcript of your coursework to the colleges or universities you have designated.

Credit For Noncollege Courses

Colleges and universities are not the only ones that offer classes. Volunteer organizations and employers often provide formal training worth college credit. The American Council on Education has two programs that assess thousands of specific courses and make recommendations on the amount of college credit they are worth. Colleges and universities accept the recommendations or use them as guidelines.

One program evaluates educational courses sponsored by government agencies, business and industry, labor unions, and professional and voluntary organizations. It is the Program on Noncollegiate Sponsored Instruction (PONSI). Some of the training seminars Alice has participated in covered topics such as food preparation, kitchen safety, and nutrition. Although she has not yet earned her GED, Alice can earn college credit because of her completion of these formal job-training seminars. The number of credits each seminar is worth does not hinge on Alice's current eligibility for college enrollment.

The other program evaluates courses offered by the Army, Navy, Air Force, Marines, Coast Guard, and Department of Defense. It is the Military Evaluations Program. Jorge has never attended college, but the engineering technology classes he completed as part of his military training are worth college credit. And as an Army veteran, Jorge is eligible for a service that takes the evaluations one step further. The Army/American Council on Education Registry Transcript System (AARTS) will provide Jorge with an individualized transcript of American Council on Education credit recommendations for all courses he completed, the military occupational specialties (MOS's) he held, and examinations he passed while in the Army. All Army and National Guard enlisted personnel and veterans who enlisted after October 1981 are eligible for the transcript. Similar services are being considered by the Navy and Marine Corps.

To obtain a free transcript, see your Army Education Center for a 5454R transcript request form. Include your name, Social Security number, basic active service date, and complete address where you want the transcript sent. Mail your request to:

AARTS Operations Center
415 McPherson Ave.
Fort Leavenworth, KS 66027-1373

Recommendations for PONSI are published in *The National Guide to Educational Credit for Training Programs*; military program recommendations are in *The Guide to the Evaluation of Educational Experiences in the Armed Forces*. See the Resources section at the end of this article for more information about these publications.

Former military personnel who took a foreign language course through the Defense Language Institute may request course transcripts by sending their name, Social Security number, course title, duration of the course, and graduation date to:

    Commandant, Defense Language Institute
    Attn: ATFL-DAA-AR
    Transcripts
    Presidio of Monterey
    Monterey, CA 93944-5006

Not all of Jorge's and Alice's courses have been assessed by the American Council on Education. Training courses that have no Council credit recommendation should still be assessed by an advisor at the schools they want to attend. Course descriptions, class notes, test scores, and other documentation may be helpful for comparing training courses to their college equivalents. An oral examination or other demonstration of competency might also be required.

There is no guarantee you will receive all the credits you are seeking – but you certainly won't if you make no attempt.

Credit By Examination

Standardized tests are the best-known method of receiving college credit without taking courses. These exams are often taken by high school students seeking advanced placement for college, but they are also available to adult learners. Testing programs and colleges and universities offer exams in a number of subjects. Two U.S. Government institutes have foreign language exams for employees that also may be worth college credit.

It is important to understand that receiving a passing score on these exams does not mean you get college credit automatically. Each school determines which test results it will accept, minimum scores required, how scores are converted for credit, and the amount of credit, if any, to be assigned. Most colleges and universities accept the American Council on Education credit recommendations, published every other year in the 250-page *Guide to Educational Credit by Examination*. For more information, contact:

    The American Council on Education
    Credit by Examination Program
    One Dupont Circle, Suite 250
    Washington, DC 20036-1193
    (202) 939-9434

Testing programs:

You might know some of the five national testing programs by their acronyms or initials: CLEP, ACT PEP: RCE, DANTES, AP, and NOCTI. (The meanings of these initialisms are explained below.) There is some overlap among programs; for example, four of them have introductory accounting exams. Since you will not be awarded credit more than once for a specific subject, you should carefully evaluate each program for the subject exams you wish to take. And before taking an exam, make sure you will be awarded credit by the college or university you plan to attend.

CLEP (College-Level Examination Program), administered by the College Board, is the most widely accepted of the national testing programs; more than 2,800 accredited schools award credit for passing exam scores. Each test covers material taught in basic undergraduate courses. There are five general exams – English composition, humanities, college mathematics, natural sciences, and social sciences and history – and many subject exams. Most exams are entirely multiple-choice, but English composition exams may include an essay section. For more information, contact:

    CLEP
    P.O. Box 6600
    Princeton, NJ 08541-6600
    (609) 771-7865

ACT PEP: RCE (American College Testing Proficiency Exam Program: Regents College Examinations) tests are given in 38 subjects within arts and sciences, business, education, and nursing. Each exam is recommended for either lower- or upper-level credit. Exams contain either objective or extended response questions, and are graded according to a standard score, letter grade, or pass/fail. Fees vary, depending on the subject and type of exam. For more information or to request free study guides, contact:

    ACT PEP: Regents College Examinations
    P.O. Box 4014
    Iowa City, IA 52243
    (319) 337-1387
    (New York State residents must contact Regents College directly.)

DANTES (Defense Activity for Nontraditional Education Support) standardized tests are developed by the Educational Testing Service for the Department of Defense. Originally administered only to military personnel, the exams have been available to the public since 1983. About 50 subject tests cover business, mathematics, social science, physical science, humanities, foreign languages, and applied technology. Most of the tests consist entirely of multiple-choice questions. Schools determine their own administering fees and testing schedules. For more information or to request free study sheets, contact:

    DANTES Program Office
    Mail Stop 31-X
    Educational Testing Service
    Princeton, NJ 08541
    1(800) 257-9484

The AP (Advanced Placement) Program is a cooperative effort between secondary schools and colleges and universities. AP exams are developed each year by committees of college and high school faculty appointed by the College Board and assisted by consultants from the Educational Testing Service. Subjects include arts and languages, natural sciences, computer science, social sciences, history, and mathematics. Most tests are 2 or 3 hours long and include both multiple-choice and essay questions. AP courses are available to help students prepare for exams, which are offered in the spring. For more information about the Advanced Placement Program, contact:

    Advanced Placement Services
    P.O. Box 6671
    Princeton, NJ 08541-6671
    (609) 771-7300

NOCTI (National Occupational Competency Testing Institute) assessments are designed for people like Alice, who have vocational-technical skills that cannot be evaluated by other tests. NOCTI assesses competency at two levels: Student/job ready and teacher/experienced worker. Standardized evaluations are available for occupations such as auto-body repair, electronics, mechanical drafting, quantity food preparation, and upholstering. The tests consist of multiple-choice questions and a performance component. Other services include workshops, customized assessments, and pre-testing. For more information, contact:

NOCTI
500 N. Bronson Ave.
Ferris State University
Big Rapids, MI 49307
(616) 796-4699

Colleges and universities:

Many colleges and universities have credit-by-exam programs, through which students earn credit by passing a comprehensive exam for a course offered by the institution. Among the most widely recognized are the programs at Ohio University, the University of North Carolina, Thomas Edison State College, and New York University.

Ohio University offers about 150 examinations for credit. In addition, you may sometimes arrange to take special examinations in non-laboratory courses offered at Ohio University. To take a test for credit, you must enroll in the course. If you plan to transfer the credit earned, you also need written permission from an official at your school. Books and study materials are available, for a cost, through the university. Exams must be taken within 6 months of the enrollment date; most last 3 hours. You may arrange to take the exam off campus if you do not live near the university.

Ohio University is on the quarter-hour system; most courses are worth 4 quarter hours, the equivalent of 3 semester hours. For more information, contact:

Independent Study
Tupper Hall 302
Ohio University
Athens, OH 45701-2979
1(800) 444-2910
(614) 593-2910

The University of North Carolina offers a credit-by-examination option for 140 independent study (correspondence) courses in foreign languages, humanities, social sciences, mathematics, business administration, education, electrical and computer engineering, health administration, and natural sciences. To take an exam, you must request and receive approval from both the course instructor and the independent studies department. Exams must be taken within six months of enrollment, and you may register for no more than two at a time. If you are not near the University's Chapel Hill campus, you may take your exam under supervision at an accredited college, university, community college, or technical institute. For more information, contact:

Independent Studies
CB #1020, The Friday Center
UNC-Chapel Hill
Chapel Hill, NC 27599-1020
1(800) 862-5669 / (919) 962-1134

The Thomas Edison College Examination Program offers more than 50 exams in liberal arts, business, and professional areas. Thomas Edison State College administers tests twice a month in Trenton, New Jersey; however, students may arrange to take their tests with a proctor at any accredited American college or university or U.S. military base. Most of the tests are multiple choice; some also include short answer or essay questions. Time limits range from 90 minutes to 4 hours, depending on the exam. For more information, contact:

Thomas Edison State College
TECEP, Office of Testing and Assessment
101 W. State Street
Trenton, NJ 08608-1176
(609) 633-2844

New York University's Foreign Language Program offers proficiency exams in more than 40 languages, from Albanian to Yiddish. Two exams are available in each language: The 12-point test is equivalent to 4 undergraduate semesters, and the 16-point exam may lead to upper level credit. The tests are given at the university's Foreign Language Department throughout the year.

Proof of foreign language proficiency does not guarantee college credit. Some colleges and universities accept transcripts only for languages commonly taught, such as French and Spanish. Nontraditional programs are more likely than traditional ones to grant credit for proficiency in other languages.

For an informational brochure and registration form for NYU's foreign language proficiency exams, contact:

New York University
Foreign Language Department
48 Cooper Square, Room 107
New York, NY 10003
(212) 998-7030

Government institutes:

The Defense Language Institute and Foreign Service Institute administer foreign language proficiency exams for personnel stationed abroad. Usually, the tests are given at the end of intensive language courses or upon completion of service overseas. But some people – like Jorge, who knows Spanish – speak another language fluently and may be allowed to take a proficiency exam in that language before completing their tour of duty. Contact one of the offices listed below to obtain transcripts of those scores. Proof of proficiency does not guarantee college credit, however, as discussed above.

To request score reports from the Defense Language Institute for Defense Language Proficiency Tests, send your name, Social Security number, language for which you were tested, and, most importantly, when and where you took the exam to:

Commandant, Defense Language Institute
Attn: ATFL-ES-T
DLPT Score Report Request
Presidio of Monterey
Monterey, CA 93944-5006

To request transcripts of scores for Foreign Service Institute exams, send your name, Social Security number, language for which you were tested, and dates or year of exams to:

Foreign Service Institute
Arlington Hall
4020 Arlington Boulevard
Rosslyn, VA 22204-1500
Attn: Testing Office (Send your request to the attention of the testing office of the foreign language in which you were tested)

Credit For Experience

Experiential learning credit may be given for knowledge gained through job responsibilities, personal hobbies, volunteer opportunities, homemaking, and other experiences. Colleges and universities base credit awards on the knowledge you have attained, not for the experience alone. In addition, the knowledge must be college level; not just any learning will do. Throwing horseshoes as a hobby is not likely to be worth college credit. But if you've done research on how and where the sport originated, visited blacksmiths, organized tournaments, and written a column for a trade journal – well, that's a horseshoe of a different color.

Adults attempting to get credit for their experience should be forewarned: Having your experience evaluated for college credit is time-consuming, tedious work – not an easy shortcut for people who want quick-fix college credits. And not all experience, no matter how valuable, is the equivalent of college courses.

Requesting college credit for your experiential learning can be tricky. You should get assistance from a credit evaluations officer at the school you plan to attend, but you should also have a general idea of what your knowledge is worth. A common method for converting knowledge into credit is to use a college catalog. Find course titles and descriptions that match what you have learned through experience, and request the number of credits offered for those courses.

Once you know what credit to ask for, you must usually present your case in writing to officials at the college you plan to attend. The most common form of presenting experiential learning for credit is the portfolio. A portfolio is a written record of your knowledge along with a request for equivalent college credit. It includes an identification and description of the knowledge for which you are requesting credit, an explanatory essay of how the knowledge was gained and how it fits into your educational plans, documentation that you have acquired such knowledge, and a request for college credit. Required elements of a portfolio vary by schools but generally follow those guidelines.

In identifying knowledge you have gained, be specific about exactly what you have learned. For example, it is not enough for Lynette to say she runs a business. She must identify the knowledge she has gained from running it, such as personnel management, tax law, marketing strategy, and inventory review. She must also include brief descriptions about her knowledge of each to support her claims of having those skills.

The essay gives you a chance to relay something about who you are. It should address your educational goals, include relevant autobiographical details, and be well organized, neat, and convey confidence. In his essay, Jorge might first state his goal of becoming an engineer. Then he would explain why he joined the Army, where he got hands-on training and experience in developing and servicing electronic equipment.

This, he would say, led to his hobby of creating remote-controlled model cars, of which he has built 20. His conclusion would highlight his accomplishments and tie them to his desire to become an electronic engineer.

Documentation is evidence that you've learned what you claim to have learned. You can show proof of knowledge in a variety of ways, including audio or video recordings, letters from current or former employers describing your specific duties and job performance, blueprints, photographs or artwork, and transcripts of certifying exams for professional licenses and certification – such as Alice's certification from the American Culinary Federation. Although documentation can take many forms, written proof alone is not always enough. If it is impossible to document your knowledge in writing, find out if your experiential learning can be assessed through supplemental oral exams by a faculty expert.

Earning a College Degree

Nontraditional students often have work, family, and financial obligations that prevent them from quitting their jobs to attend school full time. Can they still meet their educational goals? Yes.

More than 150 accredited colleges and universities have nontraditional bachelor's degree programs that require students to spend little or no time on campus; over 300 others have nontraditional campus-based degree programs. Some of those schools, as well as most junior and community colleges, offer associate's degrees nontraditionally. Each school with a nontraditional course of study determines its own rules for awarding credit for prior coursework, exams, or experience, as discussed previously. Most have charges on top of tuition for providing these special services.

Several publications profile nontraditional degree programs; see the Resources section at the end of this article for more information. To determine which school best fits your academic profile and educational goals, first list your criteria. Then, evaluate nontraditional programs based on their accreditation, features, residency requirements, and expenses. Once you have chosen several schools to explore further, write to them for more information. Detailed explanations of school policies should help you decide which ones you want to apply to.

Get beyond the printed word – especially the glowing words each school writes about itself. Check out the schools you are considering with higher education authorities, alumni, employers, family members, and friends. If possible, visit the campus to talk to students and instructors and sit in on a few classes, even if you will be completing most or all of your work off campus. Ask school officials questions about such things as enrollment numbers, graduation rate, faculty qualifications, and confusing details about the application process or academic policies. After you have thoroughly investigated each prospective college or university, you can make an informed decision about which is right for you.

Accreditation

Accreditation is a process colleges and universities submit to voluntarily for getting their credentials. An accredited school has been investigated and visited by teams of observers and has periodic inspections by a private accrediting agency. The initial review can take two years or more.

Regional agencies accredit entire schools, and professional agencies accredit either specialized schools or departments within schools. Although there are no national accrediting standards, not just any accreditation will do. Countless "accreditation associations" have been invented by schools, many of which have no academic programs and sell phony degrees, to accredit themselves. But 6 regional and about 80 professional accrediting associations in the United States are recognized by the U.S. Department of Education or the Commission on Recognition of Postsecondary Accreditation. When checking accreditation, these are the names to look for. For more information about accreditation and accrediting agencies, contact:

>Institutional Participation Oversight Service Accreditation and State Liaison Division
>U.S. Department of Education
>ROB 3, Room 3915
>600 Independence Ave., SW
>Washington, DC 20202-5244
>(202) 708-7417

Because accreditation is not mandatory, lack of accreditation does not necessarily mean a school or program is bad. Some schools choose not to apply for accreditation, are in the process of applying, or have educational methods too unconventional for an accrediting association's standards. For the nontraditional student, however, earning a degree from a college or university with recognized accreditation is an especially important consideration. Although nontraditional education is becoming more widely accepted, it is not yet mainstream. Employers skeptical of a degree earned in a nontraditional manner are likely to be even less accepting of one from an unaccredited school.

Program Features

Because nontraditional students have diverse educational objectives, nontraditional schools are diverse in what they offer. Some programs are geared toward helping students organize their scattered educational credits to get a degree as quickly as possible. Others cater to those who may have specific credits or experience but need assistance in completing requirements. Whatever your educational profile, you should look for a program that works with you in obtaining your educational goals.

A few nontraditional programs have special admissions policies for adult learners like Alice, who plan to earn their GEDs but want to enroll in college in the meantime. Other features of nontraditional programs include individualized learning agreements, intensive academic counseling, cooperative learning and internship placement, and waiver of some prerequisites or other requirements – as well as college credit for prior coursework, examinations, and experiential learning, all discussed previously.

Lynette, whose primary goal is to finish her degree, wants to earn maximum credits for her business experience. She will look for programs that do not limit the number of credits awarded for equivalency exams and experiential learning. And since well-documented proof of knowledge is essential for earning experiential learning credits, Lynette should make sure the program she chooses provides assistance to students submitting a portfolio.

Jorge, on the other hand, has more credits than he needs in certain areas and is willing to forego some. To become an engineer, he must have a bachelor's degree; but because he is accustomed to hands-on learning, Jorge is interested in getting experience as he gains more technical skills. He will concentrate on finding schools with strong cooperative education, supervised fieldwork, or internship programs.

Residency Requirements

Programs are sometimes deemed nontraditional because of their residency requirements. Many people think of residency for colleges and universities in terms of tuition, with in-state students paying less than out-of-state ones. Residency also may refer to where a student lives, either on or off campus, while attending school.

But in nontraditional education, residency usually refers to how much time students must spend on campus, regardless of whether they attend classes there. In some nontraditional programs, students need not ever step foot on campus. Others require only a very short residency, such as one day or a few weeks. Many schools have standard residency requirements of several semesters but schedule classes for evenings or weekends to accommodate working adults.

Lynette, who previously took courses by independent study, prefers to earn credits by distance study. She will focus on schools that have no residency requirement. Several colleges and universities have nonresident degree completion programs for adults with some college credit. Under the direction of a faculty advisor, students devise a plan for earning their remaining credits. Methods for earning credits include independent study, distance learning, seminars, supervised fieldwork, and group study at arranged sites. Students may have to earn a certain number of credits through the degree-granting institution. But many programs allow students to take courses at accredited schools of their choice for transfer toward their degree.

Alice wants to attend lectures but has an unpredictable schedule. Her best course of action will be to seek out short residency programs that require students to attend seminars once or twice a semester. She can take courses that are televised and videotape them to watch when her schedule permits, with the seminars helping to ensure that she properly completes her coursework. Many colleges and universities with short residency requirements also permit students to earn some credits elsewhere, by whatever means the student chooses.

Some fields of study require classroom instruction. As Jorge will discover, few colleges and universities allow students to earn a bachelor's degree in engineering entirely through independent study. Nontraditional residency programs are designed to accommodate adults' daytime work schedules. Jorge should look for programs offering evening, weekend, summer, and accelerated courses.

Tuition and Other Expenses

The final decisions about which schools Alice, Jorge, and Lynette attend may hinge in large part on a single issue: Cost. And rising tuition is only part of the equation. Beginning with application fees and continuing through graduation fees, college expenses add up.

Traditional and nontraditional students have some expenses in common, such as the cost of books and other materials. Tuition might even be the same for some courses, especially for colleges and universities offering standard ones at unusual times. But for nontraditional programs, students may also pay fees for services such as credit or transcript review, evaluation, advisement, and portfolio assessment.

Students are also responsible for postage and handling or setup expenses for independent study courses, as well as for all examination and transcript fees for transferring credits. Usually, the more nontraditional the program, the more detailed the fees. Some schools charge a yearly enrollment fee rather than tuition for degree completion candidates who want their files to remain active.

Although tuition and fees might seem expensive, most educators tell you not to let money come between you and your educational goals. Talk to someone in the financial aid department of the school you plan to attend or check your library for publications about financial aid sources. The U.S. Department of Education publishes a guide to Federal aid programs such as Pell Grants, student loans, and work-study. To order the free 74-page booklet, *The Student Guide: Financial Aid from the U.S. Department of Education,* contact:

    Federal Student Aid Information Center
    P.O. Box 84
    Washington, DC 20044
    1 (800) 4FED-AID (433-3243)

Resources

Information on how to earn a high school diploma or college degree without following the usual routes is available from several organizations and in numerous publications. Information on nontraditional graduate degree programs, available for master's through doctoral level, though not discussed in this article, can usually be obtained from the same resources that detail bachelor's degree programs.

National Learning Corporation publishes study guides for all of these exams, for both general examinations and tests in specific subject areas. To order study guides, or to browse their catalog featuring more than 5,000 titles, visit NLC online at www.passbooks.com, or contact them by phone at (800) 632-8888.

Organizations

Adult learners should always contact their local school system, community college, or university to learn about programs that are readily available. The following national organizations can also supply information:

    American Council on Education
    One Dupont Circle
    Washington, DC 20036-1193
    (202) 939-9300

Within the American Council on Education, the Center for Adult Learning and Educational Credentials administers the National External Diploma Program, the GED Program, the Program on Noncollegiate Sponsored Instruction, the Credit by Examination Program, and the Military Evaluations Program.

College-Level Examination Program (CLEP)

1. WHAT IS CLEP?

CLEP stands for the College-Level Examination Program, sponsored by the College Board. It is a national program of credit-by-examination that offers you the opportunity to obtain recognition for college-level achievement. No matter when, where, or how you have learned – by means of formal or informal study – you can take CLEP tests. If the results are acceptable to your college, you can receive credit.

You may not realize it, but you probably know more than your academic record reveals. Each day you, like most people, have an opportunity to learn. In private industry and business, as well as at all levels of government, learning opportunities continually occur. If you read widely or intensively in a particular field, think about what you read, discuss it with your family and friends, you are learning. Or you may be learning on a more formal basis by taking a correspondence course, a television or radio course, a course recorded on tape or cassettes, a course assembled into programmed tests, or a course taught in your community adult school or high school.

No matter how, where, or when you gained your knowledge, you may have the opportunity to receive academic credit for your achievement that can be counted toward an undergraduate degree. The College-Level Examination Program (CLEP) enables colleges to evaluate your achievement and give you credit. A wide range of college-level examinations are offered by CLEP to anyone who wishes to take them. Scores on the tests are reported to you and, if you wish, to a college, employer, or individual.

2. WHAT ARE THE PURPOSES OF THE COLLEGE-LEVEL EXAMINATION PROGRAM?

The basic purpose of the College-Level Examination Program is to enable individuals who have acquired their education in nontraditional ways to demonstrate their academic achievement. It is also intended for use by those in higher education, business, industry, government, and other fields who need a reliable method of assessing a person's educational level.

Recognizing that the real issue is not how a person has acquired his education but what education he has, the College Level Examination Program has been designed to serve a variety of purposes. The basic purpose, as listed above, is to enable those who have reached the college level of education in nontraditional ways to assess the level of their achievement and to use the test results in seeking college credit or placement.

In addition, scores on the tests can be used to validate educational experience obtained at a nonaccredited institution or through noncredit college courses.

Some colleges and universities may use the tests to measure the level of educational achievement of their students, and for various institutional research purposes.

Other colleges and universities may wish to use the tests in the admission, placement, and guidance of students who wish to transfer from one institution to another.

Businesses, industries, governmental agencies, and professional groups now accept the results of these tests as a basis for advancement, eligibility for further training, or professional or semi-professional certification.

Many people are interested in the examination simply to assess their own educational progress and attainment.

The college, university, business, industry, or government agency that adopts the tests in the College-Level Examination Program makes its own decision about how it will use and interpret the test scores. The College Board will provide the tests, score them, and report the results either to the individuals who took the tests or the college or agency that administered them. It does NOT, and cannot, award college credit, certify college equivalency, or make recommendations regarding the standards these institutions should establish for the use of the test results.

Therefore, if you are taking the tests to secure credit from an institution, you should FIRST ascertain whether the college or agency involved will accept the scores. Each institution determines which CLEP tests it will accept for credit and the amount of credit it will award. If you want to take tests for college credit, first call, write, or visit the college you wish to attend to inquire about its policy on CLEP scores, as well as its other admission requirements.

The services of the program are also available to people who have been requested to take the tests by an employer, a professional licensing agency, a certifying agency, or by other groups that recognize college equivalency on the basis of satisfactory CLEP scores. You may, of course, take the tests SOLELY for your own information. If you do, your scores will be reported only to you.

While neither CLEP nor the College Board can evaluate previous credentials or award college credit, you will receive, with your scores, basic information to help you interpret your performance on the tests you have taken.

3. WHAT ARE THE COLLEGE-LEVEL EXAMINATIONS?

In order to meet different kinds of curricular organization and testing needs at colleges and universities, the College-Level Examination Program offers 35 different subject tests falling under five separate general categories: Composition and Literature, Foreign Languages, History and Social Sciences, Science and Mathematics, and Business.

4. WHAT ARE THE SUBJECT EXAMINATIONS?

The 35 CLEP tests offered by the College Board are listed below:

COMPOSITION AND LITERATURE:
- American Literature
- Analyzing and Interpreting Literature
- English Composition
- English Composition with Essay
- English Literature
- Freshman College Composition
- Humanities

FOREIGN LANGUAGES
- French
- German
- Spanish

HISTORY AND SOCIAL SCIENCES
- American Government
- Introduction to Educational Psychology
- History of the United States I: Early Colonization to 1877
- History of the United States II: 1865 to the Present
- Human Growth and Development
- Principles of Macroeconomics
- Principles of Microeconomics
- Introductory Psychology
- Social Sciences and History
- Introductory Sociology
- Western Civilization I: Ancient Near East to 1648
- Western Civilization II: 1648 to the Present

SCIENCE AND MATHEMATICS
- College Algebra
- College Algebra-Trigonometry
- Biology
- Calculus
- Chemistry
- College Mathematics
- Natural Sciences
- Trigonometry
- Precalculus

BUSINESS
- Financial Accounting
- Introductory Business Law
- Information Systems and Computer Applications
- Principles of Management
- Principles of Marketing

CLEP Examinations cover material taught in courses that most students take as requirements in the first two years of college. A college usually grants the same amount of credit to students earning satisfactory scores on the CLEP examination as it grants to students successfully completing the equivalent course.

Many examinations are designed to correspond to one-semester courses; some, however, correspond to full-year or two-year courses.

Each exam is 90 minutes long and, except for English Composition with Essay, is made up primarily of multiple-choice questions. Some tests have several other types of questions besides multiple choice. To see a more detailed description of a particular CLEP exam, visit www.collegeboard.com/clep.

The English Composition with Essay exam is the only exam that includes a required essay. This essay is scored by college English faculty designated by CLEP and does not require an additional fee. However, other Composition and Literature tests offer optional essays, which some college and universities require and some do not. These essays are graded by faculty at the individual institutions that require them and require an additional $10 fee. Contact the particular institution to ask about essay requirements, and check with your test center for further details.

All 35 CLEP examinations are administered on computer. If you are unfamiliar with taking a test on a computer, consult the CLEP Sampler online at www.collegeboard.com/clep. The Sampler contains the same tutorials as the actual exams and helps familiarize you with navigation and how to answer different types of questions.

Points are not deducted for wrong or skipped answers – you receive one point for every correct answer. Therefore it is best that an answer is supplied for each exam question, whether it is a guess or not. The number of correct answers is then converted to a formula score. This formula, or "scaled," score is determined by a statistical process called *equating*, which adjusts for slight differences in difficulty between test forms and ensures that your score does not depend on the specific test form you took or how well others did on the same form. The scaled scores range from 20 to 80 – this is the number that will appear on your score report.

To ensure that you complete all questions in the time allotted, you would probably be wise to skip the more difficult or perplexing questions and return to them later. Although the multiple-choice items in these tests are carefully designed so as not to be tricky, misleading, or ambiguous, on the other hand, they are not all direct questions of factual information. They attempt, in their way, to elicit a response that indicates your knowledge or lack of knowledge of the material in question or your ability or inability to use or interpret a fact or idea. Thus, you should concentrate on answering the questions as they appear to be without attempting to out-guess the testmakers.

5. WHAT ARE THE FEES?

The fee for all CLEP examinations is $55. Optional essays required by some institutions are an additional $10.

6. WHEN ARE THE TESTS GIVEN?

CLEP tests are administered year-round. Consult the CLEP website (www.collegeboard.com/clep) and individual test centers for specific information.

7. WHERE ARE THE TESTS GIVEN?

More than 1,300 test centers are located on college and university campuses throughout the country, and additional centers are being established to meet increased needs. Any accredited collegiate institution with an explicit and publicly available policy of credit by examination can become a CLEP test center. To obtain a list of these centers, visit the CLEP website at www.collegeboard.com/clep.

8. HOW DO I REGISTER FOR THE COLLEGE-LEVEL EXAMINATION PROGRAM?

Contact an individual test center for information regarding registration, scheduling and fees. Registration/admission forms can also be obtained on the CLEP website.

9. MAY I REPEAT THE COLLEGE-LEVEL EXAMINATIONS?

You may repeat any examination providing at least six months have passed since you were last administered this test. If you repeat a test within a period of time less than six months, your scores will be cancelled and your fees forfeited. To repeat a test, check the appropriate space on the registration form.

10. WHEN MAY I EXPECT MY SCORE REPORTS?

With the exception of the English Composition with Essay exam, you should receive your score report instantly once the test is complete.

11. HOW SHOULD I PREPARE FOR THE COLLEGE-LEVEL EXAMINATIONS?

This book has been specifically designed to prepare candidates for these examinations. It will help you to consider, study, and review important content, principles, practices, procedures, problems, and techniques in the form of varied and concrete applications.

12. QUESTIONS AND ANSWERS APPEARING IN THIS PUBLICATION

The College-Level Examinations are offered by the College Board. Since copies of past examinations have not been made available, we have used equivalent materials, including questions and answers, which are highly recommended by us as an appropriate means of preparing for these examinations.

If you need additional information about CLEP Examinations, visit www.collegeboard.com/clep.

THE COLLEGE-LEVEL EXAMINATION PROGRAM

How The Program Works

CLEP examinations are administered at many colleges and universities across the country, and most institutions award college credit to those who do well on them. The examinations provide people who have acquired knowledge outside the usual educational settings the opportunity to show that they have learned college-level material without taking certain college courses.

The CLEP examinations cover material that is taught in introductory-level courses at many colleges and universities. Faculties at individual colleges review the tests to ensure that they cover the important material taught in their courses. Colleges differ in the examinations they accept; some colleges accept only two or three of the examinations while others accept nearly all of them.

Although CLEP is sponsored by the College Board and the examinations are scored by Educational Testing Service (ETS), neither of these organizations can award college credit. Only accredited colleges may grant credit toward a degree. When you take a CLEP examination, you may request that a copy of your score report be sent to the college you are attending or plan to attend. After evaluating your scores, the college will decide whether or not to award you credit for a certain course or courses, or to exempt you from them. If the college gives you credit, it will record the number of credits on your permanent record, thereby indicating that you have completed work equivalent to a course in that subject. If the college decides to grant exemption without giving you credit for a course, you will be permitted to omit a course that would normally be required of you and to take a course of your choice instead.

What the Examinations Are Like

The examinations consist mostly of multiple-choice questions to be answered within a 90-minute time limit. Additional information about each CLEP examination is given in the examination guide and on the CLEP website.

Where To Take the Examinations

CLEP examinations are administered throughout the year at the test centers of approximately 1,300 colleges and universities. On the CLEP website, you will find a list of institutions that award credit for satisfactory scores on CLEP examinations. Some colleges administer CLEP examinations to their own students only. Other institutions administer the tests to anyone who registers to take them. If your college does not administer the tests, contact the test centers in your area for information about its testing schedule.

Once you have been tested, your score report will be available instantly. CLEP scores are kept on file at ETS for 20 years; and during this period, for a small fee, you may have your transcript sent to another college or to anyone else you specify. (Your scores will never be sent to anyone without your approval.)

APPROACHING A COLLEGE ABOUT CLEP

The following sections provide a step-by-step approach to learning about the CLEP policy at a particular college or university. The person or office that can best assist students desiring CLEP credit may have a different title at each institution, but the following guidelines will lead you to information about CLEP at any institution.

Adults returning to college often benefit from special assistance when they approach a college. Opportunities for adults to return to formal learning in the classroom are now widespread, and colleges and universities have worked hard to make this a smooth process for older students. Many colleges have established special service offices that are staffed with trained professionals who understand the kinds of problems facing adults returning to college. If you think you might benefit from such assistance, be sure to find out whether these services are available at your college.

How to Apply for College Credit

STEP 1. Obtain the General Information Catalog and a copy of the CLEP policy from the colleges you are considering. If you have not yet applied for admission, ask for an admissions application form too.

Information about admissions and CLEP policies can be obtained by contacting college admissions offices or finding admissions information on the school websites. Tell the admissions officer that you are a prospective student and that you are interested in applying for admission and CLEP credit. Ask for a copy of the publication in which the college's complete CLEP policy is explained. Also get the name and the telephone number of the person to contact in case you have further questions about CLEP.

At this step, you may wish to obtain information from external degree colleges. Many adults find that such colleges suit their needs exceptionally well.

STEP 2. If you have not already been admitted to the college you are considering, look at its admission requirements for undergraduate students to see if you can qualify.

This is an important step because if you can't get into college, you can't get college credit for CLEP. Nearly all colleges require students to be admitted and to enroll in one or more courses before granting the students CLEP credit.

Virtually all public community colleges and a number of four-year state colleges have open admission policies for in-state students. This usually means that they admit anyone who has graduated from high school or has earned a high school equivalency diploma.

If you think you do not meet the admission requirements, contact the admissions office for an interview with a counselor. Colleges do sometimes make exceptions, particularly for adult applicants. State why you want the interview and ask what documents you should bring with you or send in advance. (These materials may include a high school transcript, transcript of previous college work, completed application for admission, etc.) Make an extra effort to have all the information requested in time for the interview.

During the interview, relax and be yourself. Be prepared to state honestly why you think you are ready and able to do college work. If you have already taken CLEP examinations and scored high enough to earn credit, you have shown that you are able to do college work. Mention this achievement to the admissions counselor because it may increase your chances of being accepted. If you have not taken a CLEP examination, you can still improve your chances of being accepted by describing how your job training or independent study has helped prepare you for college-level work. Tell the counselor what you have learned from your work and personal experiences.

STEP 3. Evaluate the college's CLEP policy.

Typically, a college lists all its academic policies, including CLEP policies, in its general catalog. You will probably find the CLEP policy statement under a heading such as Credit-by-Examination, Advanced Standing, Advanced Placement, or External Degree Program. These sections can usually be found in the front of the catalog.

Many colleges publish their credit-by-examination policies in a separate brochure, which is distributed through the campus testing office, counseling center, admissions office, or registrar's office. If you find a very general policy statement in the college catalog, seek clarification from one of these offices.

Review the material in the section of this guide entitled Questions to Ask About a College's CLEP Policy. Use these guidelines to evaluate the college's CLEP policy. If you have not yet taken a CLEP examination, this evaluation will help you decide which examinations to take and whether or not to take the free-response or essay portion. Because individual colleges have different CLEP policies, a review of several policies may help you decide which college to attend.

STEP 4. If you have not yet applied for admission, do so early.

Most colleges expect you to apply for admission several months before you enroll, and it is essential that you meet the published application deadlines. It takes time to process your application for admission; and if you have yet to take a CLEP examination, it will be some time before the college receives and reviews your score report. You will probably want to take some, if not all, of the CLEP examinations you are interested in before you enroll so you know which courses you need not register for. In fact, some colleges require that all CLEP scores be submitted before a student registers.

Complete all forms and include all documents requested with your application(s) for admission. Normally, an admissions decision cannot be reached until all documents have been submitted and evaluated. Unless told to do so, do not send your CLEP scores until you have been officially admitted.

STEP 5. Arrange to take CLEP examination(s) or to submit your CLEP score(s).

You may want to wait to take your CLEP examinations until you know definitely which college you will be attending. Then you can make sure you are taking tests your college will accept for credit. You will also be able to request that your scores be sent to the college, free of charge, when you take the tests.

If you have already taken CLEP examinations, but did not have a copy of your score report sent to your college, you may request the College Board to send an official transcript at any time for a small fee. Use the Transcript Request Form that was sent to you with your score report. If you do not have the form, you may find it online at www.collegeboard.com/clep.

Your CLEP scores will be evaluated, probably by someone in the admissions office, and sent to the registrar's office to be posted on your permanent record once you are enrolled. Procedures vary from college to college, but the process usually begins in the admissions office.

STEP 6. Ask to receive a written notice of the credit you receive for your CLEP score(s).

A written notice may save you problems later, when you submit your degree plan or file for graduation. In the event that there is a question about whether or not you earned CLEP credit, you will have an official record of what credit was awarded. You may also need this verification of course credit if you go for academic counseling before the credit is posted on your permanent record.

STEP 7. Before you register for courses, seek academic counseling.

A discussion with your academic advisor can prevent you from taking unnecessary courses and can tell you specifically what your CLEP credit will mean to you. This step may be accomplished at the time you enroll. Most colleges have orientation sessions for new students prior to each enrollment period. During orientation, students are usually assigned an academic advisor who then gives them individual help in developing long-range plans and a course schedule for the next semester. In conjunction with this counseling, you may be asked to take some additional tests so that you can be placed at the proper course level.

External Degree Programs

If you have acquired a considerable amount of college-level knowledge through job experience, reading, or noncredit courses, if you have accumulated college credits at a variety of colleges over a period of years, or if you prefer studying on your own rather than in a classroom setting, you may want to investigate the possibility of enrolling in an external degree program. Many colleges offer external degree programs that allow you to earn a degree by passing examinations (including CLEP), transferring credit from other colleges, and demonstrating in other ways that you have satisfied the educational requirements. No classroom attendance is required, and the programs are open to out-of-state candidates as well as residents. Thomas A. Edison State College in New Jersey and Charter Oaks College in Connecticut are fully accredited independent state colleges; the New York program is part of the state university system and is also fully accredited. If you are interested in exploring an external degree, you can write for more information to:

Charter Oak College
The Exchange, Suite 171
270 Farmington Avenue
Farmington, CT 06032-1909

Regents External Degree Program
Cultural Education Center
Empire State Plaza
Albany, New York 12230

Thomas A. Edison State College
101 West State Street
Trenton, New Jersey 08608

Many other colleges also have external degree or weekend programs. While they often require that a number of courses be taken on campus, the external degree programs tend to be more flexible in transferring credit, granting credit-by-examination, and allowing independent study than other traditional programs. When applying to a college, you may wish to ask whether it has an external degree or weekend program.

Questions to Ask About a College's CLEP Policy

Before taking CLEP examinations for the purpose of earning college credit, try to find the answers to these questions:

1. Which CLEP examinations are accepted by this college?

A college may accept some CLEP examinations for credit and not others - possibly not the one you are considering. The English faculty may decide to grant college English credit based on the CLEP English Composition examination, but not on the Freshman College Composition examination. Or, the mathematics faculty may decide to grant credit based on the College Mathematics to non-mathematics majors only, requiring majors to take an examination in algebra, trigonometry, or calculus to earn credit. For these reasons, it is important that you know the specific CLEP tests for which you can receive credit.

2. Does the college require the optional free-response (essay) section as well as the objective portion of the CLEP examination you are considering?

Knowing the answer to this question ahead of time will permit you to schedule the optional essay examination when you register to take your CLEP examination.

3. Is credit granted for specific courses? If so, which ones?

You are likely to find that credit will be granted for specific courses and the course titles will be designated in the college's CLEP policy. It is not necessary, however, that credit be granted for a specific course in order for you to benefit from your CLEP credit. For instance, at many liberal arts colleges, all students must take certain types of courses; these courses may be labeled the core curriculum, general education requirements, distribution requirements, or liberal arts requirements. The requirements are often expressed in terms of credit hours. For example, all students may be required to take at least six hours of humanities, six hours of English, three hours of mathematics, six hours of natural science, and six hours of social science, with no particular courses in these disciplines specified. In these instances, CLEP credit may be given as 6 hrs. English credit or 3 hrs. Math credit without specifying for which English or mathematics courses credit has been awarded. In order to avoid possible disappointment, you should know before taking a CLEP examination what type of credit you can receive and whether you will only be exempted from a required course but receive no credit.

4. How much credit is granted for each examination you are considering, and does the college place a limit on the total amount of CLEP credit you can earn toward your degree?

Not all colleges that grant CLEP credit award the same amount for individual tests. Furthermore, some colleges place a limit on the total amount of credit you can earn through CLEP or other examinations. Other colleges may grant you exemption but no credit toward your degree. Knowing several colleges' policies concerning these issues may help you decide which college you will attend. If you think you are capable of passing a number of CLEP examinations, you may want to attend a college that will allow you to earn credit for all or most of them. For example, the state external degree programs grant credit for most CLEP examinations (and other tests as well).

5. What is the required score for earning CLEP credit for each test you are considering?

Most colleges publish the required scores or percentile ranks for earning CLEP credit in their general catalog or in a brochure. The required score may vary from test to test, so find out the required score for each test you are considering.

6. What is the college's policy regarding prior course work in the subject in which you are considering taking a CLEP test?

Some colleges will not grant credit for a CLEP test if the student has already attempted a college-level course closely aligned with that test. For example, if you successfully completed English 101 or a comparable course on another campus, you will probably not be permitted to receive CLEP credit in that subject, too. Some colleges will not permit you to earn CLEP credit for a course that you failed.

7. Does the college make additional stipulations before credit will be granted?

It is common practice for colleges to award CLEP credit only to their enrolled students. There are other stipulations, however, that vary from college to college. For example, does the college require you to formally apply for or accept CLEP credit by completing and signing a form? Or does the college require you to validate your CLEP score by successfully completing a more advanced course in the subject? Answers to these and other questions will help to smooth the process of earning college credit through CLEP.

The above questions and the discussions that follow them indicate some of the ways in which colleges' CLEP policies can vary. Find out as much as possible about the CLEP policies at the colleges you are interested in so you can choose a college with a policy that is compatible with your educational goals. Once you have selected the college you will attend, you can find out which CLEP examinations your college recognizes and the requirements for earning CLEP credit.

DECIDING WHICH EXAMINATIONS TO TAKE

If You're Taking the Examinations for College Credit or Career Advancement:

Most people who take CLEP examinations do so in order to earn credit for college courses. Others take the examinations in order to qualify for job promotions or for professional certification or licensing. It is vital to most candidates who are taking the tests for any of these reasons that they be well prepared for the tests they are taking so that they can advance as rapidly as possible toward their educational or career goals.

It is usually advisable that those who have limited knowledge in the subjects covered by the tests they are considering enroll in the college courses in which that material is taught. Those who are uncertain about whether or not they know enough about a subject to do well on a particular CLEP test will find the following guidelines helpful.

There is no way to predict if you will pass a particular CLEP examination, but answers to the questions under the seven headings below should give you an indication of whether or not you are likely to succeed.

1. Test Descriptions

Read the description of the test provided. Are you familiar with most of the topics and terminology in the outline?

2. Textbooks

Examine the suggested textbooks and other resource materials following the test descriptions in this guide. Have you recently read one or more of these books, or have you read similar college-level books on this subject? If you have not, read through one or more of the textbooks listed, or through the textbook used for this course at your college. Are you familiar with most of the topics and terminology in the book?

3. Sample Questions

The sample questions provided are intended to be typical of the content and difficulty of the questions on the test. Although they are not an exact miniature of the test, the proportion of the sample questions you can answer correctly should be a rough estimate of the proportion of questions you will be able to answer correctly on the test.

Answer as many of the sample questions for this test as you can. Check your answers against the correct answers. Did you answer more than half the questions correctly?

Because of variations in course content at different institutions, and because questions on CLEP tests vary from easy to difficult - with most being of moderate difficulty - the average student who passes a course in a subject can usually answer correctly about half the questions on the corresponding CLEP examination. Most colleges set their passing scores near this level, but some set them higher. If your college has set its required score above the level required by most colleges, you may need to answer a larger proportion of questions on the test correctly.

4. Previous Study

Have you taken noncredit courses in this subject offered by an adult school or a private school, through correspondence, or in connection with your job? Did you do exceptionally well in this subject in high school, or did you take an honors course in this subject?

5. Experience

Have you learned or used the knowledge or skills included in this test in your job or life experience? For example, if you lived in a Spanish-speaking country and spoke the language for a year or more, you might consider taking the Spanish examination. Or, if you have worked at a job in which you used accounting and finance skills, Principles of Accounting would be a likely test for you to take. Or, if you have read a considerable amount of literature and attended many art exhibits, concerts, and plays, you might expect to do well on the Humanities exam.

6. Other Examinations

Have you done well on other standardized tests in subjects related to the one you want to take? For example, did you score well above average on a portion of a college entrance examination covering similar skills, or did you obtain an exceptionally high score on a high school equivalency test or a licensing examination in this subject? Although such tests do not cover exactly the same material as the CLEP examinations and may be easier, persons who do well on these tests often do well on CLEP examinations, too.

7. Advice

Has a college counselor, professor, or some other professional person familiar with your ability advised you to take a CLEP examination?

If your answer was yes to questions under several of the above headings, you probably have a good chance of passing the CLEP examination you are considering. It is unlikely that you would have acquired sufficient background from experience alone. Learning gained through reading and study is essential, and you will probably find some additional study helpful before taking a CLEP examination.

If You're Taking the Examinations to Prepare for College

Many people entering college, particularly adults returning to college after several years away from formal education, are uncertain about their ability to compete with other college students. They wonder whether they have sufficient background for college study, and those who have been away from formal study for some time wonder whether they have forgotten how to study, how to take tests, and how to write papers. Such people may wish to improve their test-taking and study skills prior to enrolling in courses.

One way to assess your ability to perform at the college level and to improve your test-taking and study skills at the same time is to prepare for and take one or more CLEP examinations. You need not be enrolled in a college to take a CLEP examination, and you may have your scores sent only to yourself and later request that a transcript be sent to a college if you then decide to apply for credit. By reviewing the test descriptions and sample questions, you may find one or several subject areas in which you think you have substantial knowledge. Select one examination, or more if you like, and carefully read at least one of the textbooks listed in the bibliography for the test. By doing this, you will get a better idea of how much you know of what is usually taught in a college-level course in that subject. Study as much material as you can, until you think you have a good grasp of the subject matter. Then take the test at a college in your area. It will be several weeks before you receive your results, and you may wish to begin reviewing for another test in the meantime.

To find out if you are eligible for credit for your CLEP score, you must compare your score with the score required by the college you plan to attend. If you are not yet sure which college you will attend, or whether you will enroll in college at all, you should begin to follow the steps outlined. It is best that you do this before taking a CLEP test, but if you are taking the test only for the experience and to familiarize yourself with college-level material and requirements, you might take the test before you approach a college. Even if the college you decide to attend does not accept the test you took, the experience of taking such a test will enable you to meet with greater confidence the requirements of courses you will take.

You will find information about how to interpret your scores in WHAT YOUR SCORES MEAN, which you will receive with your score report, and which can also be found online at the CLEP website. Many colleges follow the recommendations of the American Council on Education (ACE) for setting their required scores, so you can use this information as a guide in determining how well you did. The ACE recommendations are included in the booklet.

If you do not do well enough on the test to earn college credit, don't be discouraged. Usually, it is the best college students who are exempted from courses or receive credit-by-examination. The fact that you cannot get credit for your score means that you should probably enroll in a college course to learn the material. However, if your score was close to the required score, or if you feel you could do better on a second try or after some additional study, you may retake the test after six months. Do not take it sooner or your score will not be reported and your fee will be forfeited.

If you do earn the score required to earn credit, you will have demonstrated that you already have some college-level knowledge. You will also have a better idea whether you should take additional CLEP examinations. And, what is most important, you can enroll in college with confidence, knowing that you do have the ability to succeed.

PREPARING TO TAKE CLEP EXAMINATIONS

Having made the decision to take one or more CLEP examinations, most people then want to know if it is worthwhile to prepare for them - how much, how long, when, and how should they go about it? The precise answers to these questions vary greatly from individual to individual. However, most candidates find that some type of test preparation is helpful.

Most people who take CLEP examinations do so to show that they have already learned the important material that is taught in a college course. Many of them need only a quick review to assure themselves that they have not forgotten some of what they once studied, and to fill in some of the gaps in their knowledge of the subject. Others feel that they need a thorough review and spend several weeks studying for a test. A few wish to take a CLEP examination as a kind of final examination for independent study of a subject instead of the college course. This last group requires significantly more study than those who only need to review, and they may need some guidance from professors of the subjects they are studying.

The key to how you prepare for CLEP examinations often lies in locating those skills and areas of prior learning in which you are strong and deciding where to focus your energies. Some people may know a great deal about a certain subject area, but may not test well. These individuals would probably be just as concerned about strengthening their test-taking skills as they are about studying for a specific test. Many mental and physical skills are used in preparing for a test. It is important not only to review or study for the examinations, but to make certain that you are alert, relatively free of anxiety, and aware of how to approach standardized tests. Suggestions on developing test-taking skills and preparing psychologically and physically for a test are given. The following section suggests ways of assessing your knowledge of the content of a test and then reviewing and studying the material.

Using This Study Guide

Begin by carefully reading the test description and outline of knowledge and skills required for the examination, if given. As you read through the topics listed there, ask yourself how much you know about each one. Also note the terms, names, and symbols that are mentioned, and ask yourself whether you are familiar with them. This will give you a quick overview of how much you know about the subject. If you are familiar with nearly all the material, you will probably need a minimum of review; however, if less than half of it is familiar, you will probably require substantial study to do well on the test.

If, after reviewing the test description, you find that you need extensive review, delay answering the sample question until you have done some reading in the subject. If you complete them before reviewing the material, you will probably look for the answers as you study, and then they will not be a good assessment of your ability at a later date.

If you think you are familiar with most of the test material, try to answer the sample questions.

Apply the test-taking strategies given. Keeping within the time limit suggested will give you a rough idea of how quickly you should work in order to complete the actual test.

Check your answers against the answer key. If you answered nearly all the questions correctly, you probably do not need to study the subject extensively. If you got about half the questions correct, you ought o review at least one textbook or other suggested materials on the subject. If you answered less than half the questions correctly, you will probably benefit from more extensive reading in the subject and thorough study of one or more textbooks. The textbooks listed are used at many colleges but they are not the only good texts. You will find helpful almost any standard text available to you., such as the textbook used at your college, or earlier editions of texts listed. For some examinations, topic outlines and textbooks may not be available. Take the sample tests in this book and check your answers at the end of each test. Check wrong answers.

Suggestions for Studying

The following suggestions have been gathered from people who have prepared for CLEP examinations or other college-level tests.

1. Define your goals and locate study materials

First, determine your study goals. Set aside a block of time to review the material provided in this book, and then decide which test(s) you will take. Using the suggestions, locate suitable resource materials. If a preparation course is offered by an adult school or college in your area, you might find it helpful to enroll.

2. Find a good place to study

To determine what kind of place you need for studying, ask yourself questions such as: Do I need a quiet place? Does the telephone distract me? Do objects I see in this place remind me of things I should do? Is it too warm? Is it well lit? Am I too comfortable here? Do I have space to spread out my materials? You may find the library more conducive to studying than your home. If you decide to study at home, you might prevent interruptions by other household members by putting a sign on the door of your study room to indicate when you will be available.

3. Schedule time to study

To help you determine where studying best fits into your schedule, try this exercise: Make a list of your daily activities (for example, sleeping, working, and eating) and estimate how many hours per day you spend on each activity. Now, rate all the activities on your list in order of their importance and evaluate your use of time. Often people are astonished at how an average day appears from this perspective. They may discover that they were unaware how large portions of time are spent, or they learn their time can be scheduled in alternative ways. For example, they can remove the least important activities from their day and devote that time to studying or another important activity.

4. Establish a study routine and a set of goals

In order to study effectively, you should establish specific goals and a schedule for accomplishing them. Some people find it helpful to write out a weekly schedule and cross out each study period when it is completed. Others maintain their concentration better by writing down the time when they expect to complete a study task. Most people find short periods of intense study more productive than long stretches of time. For example, they may follow a regular schedule of several 20- or 30-minute study periods with short breaks between them. Some people like to allow themselves rewards as they complete each study goal. It is not essential that you accomplish every goal exactly within your schedule; the point is to be committed to your task.

5. Learn how to take an active role in studying.

If you have not done much studying for some time, you may find it difficult to concentrate at first. Try a method of studying, such as the one outlined below, that will help you concentrate on and remember what you read.

    a. First, read the chapter summary and the introduction. Then you will know what to look for in your reading.

    b. Next, convert the section or paragraph headlines into questions. For example, if you are reading a section entitled, The Causes of the American Revolution, ask yourself: *What were the causes of the American Revolution?* Compose the answer as you read the paragraph. Reading and answering questions aloud will help you understand and remember the material.

c. Take notes on key ideas or concepts as you read. Writing will also help you fix concepts more firmly in your mind. Underlining key ideas or writing notes in your book can be helpful and will be useful for review. Underline only important points. If you underline more than a third of each paragraph, you are probably underlining too much.

d. If there are questions or problems at the end of a chapter, answer or solve them on paper as if you were asked to do them for homework. Mathematics textbooks (and some other books) sometimes include answers to some or all of the exercises. If you have such a book, write your answers before looking at the ones given. When problem-solving is involved, work enough problems to master the required methods and concepts. If you have difficulty with problems, review any sample problems or explanations in the chapter.

e. To retain knowledge, most people have to review the material periodically. If you are preparing for a test over an extended period of time, review key concepts and notes each week or so. Do not wait for weeks to review the material or you will need to relearn much of it.

Psychological and Physical Preparation

Most people feel at least some nervousness before taking a test. Adults who are returning to college may not have taken a test in many years or they may have had little experience with standardized tests. Some younger students, as well, are uncomfortable with testing situations. People who received their education in countries outside the United States may find that many tests given in this country are quite different from the ones they are accustomed to taking.

Not only might candidates find the types of tests and the kinds of questions on them unfamiliar, but other aspects of the testing environment may be strange as well. The physical and mental stress that results from meeting this new experience can hinder a candidate's ability to demonstrate his or her true degree of knowledge in the subject area being tested. For this reason, it is important to go to the test center well prepared, both mentally and physically, for taking the test. You may find the following suggestions helpful.

1. Familiarize yourself, as much as possible, with the test and the test situation before the day of the examination. It will be helpful for you to know ahead of time:

a. How much time will be allowed for the test and whether there are timed subsections.

b. What types of questions and directions appear on the examination.

c. How your test score will be computed.

d. How to properly answer the questions on the computer (See the CLEP Sample on the CLEP website)

    e. In which building and room the examination will be administered. If you don't know where the building is, locate it or get directions ahead of time.

    f. The time of the test administration. You might wish to confirm this information a day or two before the examination and find out what time the building and room will be open so that you can plan to arrive early.

    g. Where to park your car or, if you wish to take public transportation, which bus or train to take and the location of the nearest stop.

    h. Whether smoking will be permitted during the test.

    i. Whether there will be a break between examinations (if you will be taking more than one on the same day), and whether there is a place nearby where you can get something to eat or drink.

2. Go to the test situation relaxed and alert. In order to prepare for the test:

    a. Get a good night's sleep. Last minute cramming, particularly late the night before, is usually counterproductive.

    b. Eat normally. It is usually not wise to skip breakfast or lunch on the day of the test or to eat a big meal just before the test.

    c. Avoid tranquilizers and stimulants. If you follow the other directions in this book, you won't need artificial aids. It's better to be a little tense than to be drowsy, but stimulants such as coffee and cola can make you nervous and interfere with your concentration.

    d. Don't drink a lot of liquids before the test. Having to leave the room during the test will disturb your concentration and take valuable time away from the test.

    e. If you are inclined to be nervous or tense, learn some relaxation exercises and use them before and perhaps during the test.

3. Arrive for the test early and prepared. Be sure to:

    a. Arrive early enough so that you can find a parking place, locate the test center, and get settled comfortably before testing begins. Allow some extra time in case you are delayed unexpectedly.

    b. Take the following with you:

- Your completed Registration/Admission Form
- Two forms of identification – one being a government-issued photo ID with signature, such as a driver's license or passport
- Non-mechanical pencil
- A watch so that you can time your progress (digital watches are prohibited)
- Your glasses if you need them for reading or seeing the chalkboard or wall clock

c. Leave all books, papers, and notes outside the test center. You will not be permitted to use your own scratch paper; it will be provided. Also prohibited are calculators, cell phones, beepers, pagers, photo/copy devices, radios, headphones, food, beverages, and several other items.

d. Be prepared for any temperature in the testing room. Wear layers of clothing that can be removed if the room is too hot but will keep you warm if it is too cold.

4. When you enter the test room:

a. Sit in a seat that provides a maximum of comfort and freedom from distraction.

b. Read directions carefully, and listen to all instructions given by the test administrator. If you don't understand the directions, ask for help before test timing begins. If you must ask a question after the test has begun, raise your hand and a proctor will assist you. The proctor can answer certain kinds of questions but cannot help you with the test.

c. Know your rights as a test taker. You can expect to be given the full working time allowed for the test(s) and a reasonably quiet and comfortable place in which to work. If a poor test situation is preventing you from doing your best, ask if the situation can be remedied. If bad test conditions cannot be remedied, ask the person in charge to report the problem in the Irregularity Report that will be sent to ETS with the answer sheets. You may also wish to contact CLEP. Describe the exact circumstances as completely as you can. Be sure to include the test date and name(s) of the test(s) you took. ETS will investigate the problem to make sure it does not happen again, and, if the problem is serious enough, may arrange for you to retake the test without charge.

TAKING THE EXAMINATIONS

A person may know a great deal about the subject being tested, but not do as well as he or she is capable of on the test. Knowing how to approach a test is an important part of the testing process. While a command of test-taking skills cannot substitute for knowledge of the subject matter, it can be a significant factor in successful testing.

Test-taking skills enable a person to use all available information to earn a score that truly reflects his or her ability. There are different strategies for approaching different kinds of test questions. For example, free-response questions require a very different tack than do multiple-choice questions. Other factors, such as how the test will be graded, may also influence your approach to the test and your use of test time. Thus, your preparation for a test should include finding out all you can about the test so that you can use the most effective test-taking strategies.

Before taking a test, you should know approximately how many questions are on the test, how much time you will be allowed, how the test will be scored or graded, what types of questions and directions are on the test, and how you will be required to record your answers.

Taking Multiple-Choice Tests

1. Listen carefully to the instructions given by the test administrator and read carefully all directions before you begin to answer the questions.

2. Note the time that the test administrator starts timing the test. As you proceed, make sure that you are not working too slowly. You should have answered at least half the questions in a section when half the time for that section has passed. If you have not reached that point in the section, speed up your pace on the remaining questions.

3. Before answering a question, read the entire question, including all the answer choices. Don't think that because the first or second answer choice looks good to you, it isn't necessary to read the remaining options. Instructions usually tell you to select the best answer. Sometimes one answer choice is partially correct, but another option is better; therefore, it is usually a good idea to read all the answers before you choose one.

4. Read and consider every question. Questions that look complicated at first glance may not actually be so difficult once you have read them carefully.

5. Do not puzzle too long over any one question. If you don't know the answer after you've considered it briefly, go on to the next question. Make sure you return to the question later.

6. Make sure you record your response properly.

7. In trying to determine the correct answer, you may find it helpful to cross out those options that you know are incorrect, and to make marks next to those you think might be correct. If you decide to skip the question and come back to it later, you will save yourself the time of reconsidering all the options.

8. Watch for the following key words in test questions:

all	generally	never	perhaps
always	however	none	rarely
but	may	not	seldom
except	must	often	sometimes
every	necessary	only	usually

When a question or answer option contains words such as always, every, only, never, and none, there can be no exceptions to the answer you choose. Use of words such as often, rarely, sometimes, and generally indicates that there may be some exceptions to the answer.

9. Do not waste your time looking for clues to right answers based on flaws in question wording or patterns in correct answers. Professionals at the College Board and ETS put

a great deal of effort into developing valid, reliable, fair tests. CLEP test development committees are composed of college faculty who are experts in the subject covered by the test and are appointed by the College Board to write test questions and to scrutinize each question that is included on a CLEP test. Committee members make every effort to ensure that the questions are not ambiguous, that they have only one correct answer, and that they cover college-level topics. These committees do not intentionally include trick questions. If you think a question is flawed, ask the test administrator to report it, or contact CLEP immediately.

Taking Free-Response or Essay Tests

If your college requires the optional free-response or essay portion of a CLEP Composition and Literature exams, you should do some additional preparation for your CLEP test. Taking an essay test is very different from taking a multiple-choice test, so you will need to use some other strategies.

The essay written as part of the English Composition and Essay exam is graded by English professors from a variety of colleges and universities. A process called holistic scoring is used to rate your writing ability.

The optional free-response essays, on the other hand, are graded by the faculty of the college you designate as a score recipient. Guidelines and criteria for grading essays are not specified by the College Board or ETS. You may find it helpful, therefore, to talk with someone at your college to find out what criteria will be used to determine whether you will get credit. If the test requires essay responses, ask how much emphasis will be placed on your writing ability and your ability to organize your thoughts as opposed to your knowledge of subject matter. Find out how much weight will be given to your multiple-choice test score in comparison with your free-response grade in determining whether you will get credit. This will give you an idea where you should expend the greatest effort in preparing for and taking the test.

Here are some strategies you will find useful in taking any essay test:

1. Before you begin to write, read all questions carefully and take a few minutes to jot down some ideas you might include in each answer.

2. If you are given a choice of questions to answer, choose the questions you think you can answer most clearly and knowledgeably.

3. Determine in what order you will answer the questions. Answer those you find the easiest first so that any extra time can be spent on the more difficult questions.

4. When you know which questions you will answer and in what order, determine how much testing time remains and estimate how many minutes you will devote to each question. Unless suggested times are given for the questions or one question appears to require more or less time than the others, allot an equal amount of time to each question.

5. Before answering each question, indicate the number of the question as it is given in the test book. You need not copy the entire question from the question sheet, but it will be helpful to you and to the person grading your test if you indicate briefly the topic you are addressing – particularly if you are not answering the questions in the order in which they appear on the test.

6. Before answering each question, read it again carefully to make sure you are interpreting it correctly. Underline key words, such as those listed below, that often appear in free-response questions. Be sure you know the exact meaning of these words before taking the test.

analyze	demonstrate	enumerate	list
apply	derive	explain	outline
assess	describe	generalize	prove
compare	determine	illustrate	rank
contrast	discuss	interpret	show
define	distinguish	justify	summarize

If a question asks you to outline, define, or summarize, do not write a detailed explanation; if a question asks you to analyze, explain, illustrate, interpret, or show, you must do more than briefly describe the topic.

For a current listing of CLEP Colleges

where you can get credit and be tested, write:

CLEP, P.O. Box 6600, Princeton, NJ 08541-6600

Or e-mail: clep@ets.org, or call: (609) 771-7865

Human Growth and Development

Description of the Examination
The Human Growth and Development examination (Infancy, Childhood, Adolescence, Adulthood, and Aging) covers material that is generally taught in a one-semester introductory course in developmental psychology or human development. An understanding of the major theories and research related to the broad categories of physical development, cognitive development, and social development is required, as is the ability to apply this knowledge.

The examination contains approximately 90 questions to be answered in 90 minutes. Some of them are pretest questions that will not be scored. Any time candidates spend on tutorials and providing personal information is in addition to the actual testing time.

Knowledge and Skills Required
Questions on the Human Growth and Development examination require candidates to demonstrate one or more of the following abilities.

- Knowledge of basic facts and terminology
- Understanding of generally accepted concepts and principles
- Understanding of theories and recurrent developmental issues
- Applications of knowledge to particular problems or situations

The subject matter of the Human Growth and Development examination is drawn from the following categories. For each category, several key words and phrases identify topics with which candidates should be familiar. The percentages next to the main categories indicate the approximate percentage of exam questions on that topic.

10% Theoretical Perspectives
- Cognitive developmental
- Evolutionary
- Learning
- Psychodynamic
- Social cognitive
- Sociocultural

5% Research Strategies and Methodology
- Case study
- Correlational
- Cross-sectional
- Cross sequential
- Experimental
- Longitudinal
- Observational

10% **Biological Development Throughout the Life Span**
- Development of the brain and nervous system
- Heredity, genetics, and genetic testing
- Hormonal influences
- Influences of drugs
- Motor development
- Nutritional influences
- Perinatal influences
- Physical growth and maturation, aging
- Prenatal influences
- Sexual maturation
- Teratogens

7% **Perceptual Development Throughout the Life Span**
- Sensitive periods
- Sensorimotor activities
- Sensory acuity
- Sensory deprivation

12% **Cognitive Development Throughout the Life Span**
- Attention
- Environmental influences
- Executive function
- Expertise
- Information processing
- Memory
- Piaget, Jean
- Play
- Problem solving and planning
- Thinking
- Vygotsky, Lev
- Wisdom

8% **Language Development**
- Bilingualism
- Development of syntax
- Environmental, cultural, and genetic influences
- Language and thought
- Pragmatics
- Semantic development
- Vocalization and sound

4% **Intelligence Throughout the Life Span**
- Concepts of intelligence and creativity
- Developmental stability and change
- Heredity and environment

10%   **Social Development Throughout the Life Span**
- Aggression
- Attachment
- Gender
- Interpersonal relationships
- Moral development
- Prosocial behavior
- Risk and resilience
- Self
- Social cognition
- Wellness

8%   **Family, Home, and Society Throughout the Life Span**
- Abuse and neglect
- Bronfenbrenner, Urie
- Death and dying
- Family relationships
- Family structures
- Media and technology
- Multicultural perspectives
- Parenting styles
- Social and class influences

8%   **Personality and Emotion**
- Attribution styles
- Development of emotions
- Emotional expression and regulation
- Emotional intelligence
- Erikson, Erik
- Freud, Sigmund
- Stability and change
- Temperament

8%   **Learning**
- Classical conditioning
- Discrimination and generalization
- Habituation
- Operant conditioning
- Social learning and modeling

5%   **Schooling, Work, and Interventions**
- Applications of developmental principles
- Facilitation of role transitions
- Intervention programs and services
- Learning styles
- Occupational development
- Preschool care, day care, and elder care
- Retirement

5% **Atypical Development**
- Antisocial behavior
- Asocial behavior, fears, phobias, and obsessions
- Attention-deficit/hyperactivity disorder
- Autism spectrum disorders
- Chronic illnesses and physical disabilities
- Cognitive disorders, including dementia
- Genetic disorders
- Giftedness
- Learning disabilities
- Mental retardation
- Mood disorders
- Trauma-based syndromes

HOW TO TAKE A TEST

You have studied long, hard and conscientiously.

With your official admission card in hand, and your heart pounding, you have been admitted to the examination room.

You note that there are several hundred other applicants in the examination room waiting to take the same test.

They all appear to be equally well prepared.

You know that nothing but your best effort will suffice. The "moment of truth" is at hand: you now have to demonstrate objectively, in writing, your knowledge of content and your understanding of subject matter.

You are fighting the most important battle of your life—to pass and/or score high on an examination which will determine your career and provide the economic basis for your livelihood.

What extra, special things should you know and should you do in taking the examination?

I. YOU MUST PASS AN EXAMINATION

A. WHAT EVERY CANDIDATE SHOULD KNOW
Examination applicants often ask us for help in preparing for the written test. What can I study in advance? What kinds of questions will be asked? How will the test be given? How will the papers be graded?

B. HOW ARE EXAMS DEVELOPED?
Examinations are carefully written by trained technicians who are specialists in the field known as "psychological measurement," in consultation with recognized authorities in the field of work that the test will cover. These experts recommend the subject matter areas or skills to be tested; only those knowledges or skills important to your success on the job are included. The most reliable books and source materials available are used as references. Together, the experts and technicians judge the difficulty level of the questions.
Test technicians know how to phrase questions so that the problem is clearly stated. Their ethics do not permit "trick" or "catch" questions. Questions may have been tried out on sample groups, or subjected to statistical analysis, to determine their usefulness.
Written tests are often used in combination with performance tests, ratings of training and experience, and oral interviews. All of these measures combine to form the best-known means of finding the right person for the right job.

II. HOW TO PASS THE WRITTEN TEST

A. BASIC STEPS

1) Study the announcement

How, then, can you know what subjects to study? Our best answer is: "Learn as much as possible about the class of positions for which you've applied." The exam will test the knowledge, skills and abilities needed to do the work.

Your most valuable source of information about the position you want is the official exam announcement. This announcement lists the training and experience qualifications. Check these standards and apply only if you come reasonably close to meeting them. Many jurisdictions preview the written test in the exam announcement by including a section called "Knowledge and Abilities Required," "Scope of the Examination," or some similar heading. Here you will find out specifically what fields will be tested.

2) Choose appropriate study materials

If the position for which you are applying is technical or advanced, you will read more advanced, specialized material. If you are already familiar with the basic principles of your field, elementary textbooks would waste your time. Concentrate on advanced textbooks and technical periodicals. Think through the concepts and review difficult problems in your field.

These are all general sources. You can get more ideas on your own initiative, following these leads. For example, training manuals and publications of the government agency which employs workers in your field can be useful, particularly for technical and professional positions. A letter or visit to the government department involved may result in more specific study suggestions, and certainly will provide you with a more definite idea of the exact nature of the position you are seeking.

3) Study this book!

III. KINDS OF TESTS

Tests are used for purposes other than measuring knowledge and ability to perform specified duties. For some positions, it is equally important to test ability to make adjustments to new situations or to profit from training. In others, basic mental abilities not dependent on information are essential. Questions which test these things may not appear as pertinent to the duties of the position as those which test for knowledge and information. Yet they are often highly important parts of a fair examination. For very general questions, it is almost impossible to help you direct your study efforts. What we can do is to point out some of the more common of these general abilities needed in public service positions and describe some typical questions.

1) General information

Broad, general information has been found useful for predicting job success in some kinds of work. This is tested in a variety of ways, from vocabulary lists to questions about current events. Basic background in some field of work, such as sociology or economics, may be sampled in a group of questions. Often these are principles which have become familiar to most persons through exposure rather than through formal training. It is difficult to advise you how to study for these questions; being alert to the world around you is our best suggestion.

2) Verbal ability

An example of an ability needed in many positions is verbal or language ability. Verbal ability is, in brief, the ability to use and understand words. Vocabulary and grammar tests are typical measures of this ability. Reading comprehension or paragraph interpretation questions are common in many kinds of civil service tests. You are given a paragraph of written material and asked to find its central meaning.

IV. KINDS OF QUESTIONS

1. Multiple-choice Questions

Most popular of the short-answer questions is the "multiple choice" or "best answer" question. It can be used, for example, to test for factual knowledge, ability to solve problems or judgment in meeting situations found at work.

A multiple-choice question is normally one of three types:
- It can begin with an incomplete statement followed by several possible endings. You are to find the one ending which best completes the statement, although some of the others may not be entirely wrong.
- It can also be a complete statement in the form of a question which is answered by choosing one of the statements listed.
- It can be in the form of a problem – again you select the best answer.

Here is an example of a multiple-choice question with a discussion which should give you some clues as to the method for choosing the right answer:

When an employee has a complaint about his assignment, the action which will best help him overcome his difficulty is to
- A. discuss his difficulty with his coworkers
- B. take the problem to the head of the organization
- C. take the problem to the person who gave him the assignment
- D. say nothing to anyone about his complaint

In answering this question, you should study each of the choices to find which is best. Consider choice "A" – Certainly an employee may discuss his complaint with fellow employees, but no change or improvement can result, and the complaint remains unresolved. Choice "B" is a poor choice since the head of the organization probably does not know what assignment you have been given, and taking your problem to him is known as "going over the head" of the supervisor. The supervisor, or person who made the assignment, is the person who can clarify it or correct any injustice. Choice "C" is, therefore, correct. To say nothing, as in choice "D," is unwise. Supervisors have and interest in knowing the problems employees are facing, and the employee is seeking a solution to his problem.

2. True/False

3. Matching Questions

Matching an answer from a column of choices within another column.

V. RECORDING YOUR ANSWERS

Computer terminals are used more and more today for many different kinds of exams.

For an examination with very few applicants, you may be told to record your answers in the test booklet itself. Separate answer sheets are much more common. If this separate answer sheet is to be scored by machine – and this is often the case – it is highly important that you mark your answers correctly in order to get credit.

VI. BEFORE THE TEST

YOUR PHYSICAL CONDITION IS IMPORTANT

If you are not well, you can't do your best work on tests. If you are half asleep, you can't do your best either. Here are some tips:

1) Get about the same amount of sleep you usually get. Don't stay up all night before the test, either partying or worrying—DON'T DO IT!
2) If you wear glasses, be sure to wear them when you go to take the test. This goes for hearing aids, too.
3) If you have any physical problems that may keep you from doing your best, be sure to tell the person giving the test. If you are sick or in poor health, you relay cannot do your best on any test. You can always come back and take the test some other time.

Common sense will help you find procedures to follow to get ready for an examination. Too many of us, however, overlook these sensible measures. Indeed, nervousness and fatigue have been found to be the most serious reasons why applicants fail to do their best on civil service tests. Here is a list of reminders:

- Begin your preparation early – Don't wait until the last minute to go scurrying around for books and materials or to find out what the position is all about.
- Prepare continuously – An hour a night for a week is better than an all-night cram session. This has been definitely established. What is more, a night a week for a month will return better dividends than crowding your study into a shorter period of time.
- Locate the place of the exam – You have been sent a notice telling you when and where to report for the examination. If the location is in a different town or otherwise unfamiliar to you, it would be well to inquire the best route and learn something about the building.
- Relax the night before the test – Allow your mind to rest. Do not study at all that night. Plan some mild recreation or diversion; then go to bed early and get a good night's sleep.
- Get up early enough to make a leisurely trip to the place for the test – This way unforeseen events, traffic snarls, unfamiliar buildings, etc. will not upset you.
- Dress comfortably – A written test is not a fashion show. You will be known by number and not by name, so wear something comfortable.
- Leave excess paraphernalia at home – Shopping bags and odd bundles will get in your way. You need bring only the items mentioned in the official notice you received; usually everything you need is provided. Do not bring reference books to the exam. They will only confuse those last minutes and be taken away from you when in the test room.

- Arrive somewhat ahead of time – If because of transportation schedules you must get there very early, bring a newspaper or magazine to take your mind off yourself while waiting.
- Locate the examination room – When you have found the proper room, you will be directed to the seat or part of the room where you will sit. Sometimes you are given a sheet of instructions to read while you are waiting. Do not fill out any forms until you are told to do so; just read them and be prepared.
- Relax and prepare to listen to the instructions
- If you have any physical problem that may keep you from doing your best, be sure to tell the test administrator. If you are sick or in poor health, you really cannot do your best on the exam. You can come back and take the test some other time.

VII. AT THE TEST

The day of the test is here and you have the test booklet in your hand. The temptation to get going is very strong. Caution! There is more to success than knowing the right answers. You must know how to identify your papers and understand variations in the type of short-answer question used in this particular examination. Follow these suggestions for maximum results from your efforts:

1) Cooperate with the monitor

The test administrator has a duty to create a situation in which you can be as much at ease as possible. He will give instructions, tell you when to begin, check to see that you are marking your answer sheet correctly, and so on. He is not there to guard you, although he will see that your competitors do not take unfair advantage. He wants to help you do your best.

2) Listen to all instructions

Don't jump the gun! Wait until you understand all directions. In most civil service tests you get more time than you need to answer the questions. So don't be in a hurry. Read each word of instructions until you clearly understand the meaning. Study the examples, listen to all announcements and follow directions. Ask questions if you do not understand what to do.

3) Identify your papers

Civil service exams are usually identified by number only. You will be assigned a number; you must not put your name on your test papers. Be sure to copy your number correctly. Since more than one exam may be given, copy your exact examination title.

4) Plan your time

Unless you are told that a test is a "speed" or "rate of work" test, speed itself is usually not important. Time enough to answer all the questions will be provided, but this does not mean that you have all day. An overall time limit has been set. Divide the total time (in minutes) by the number of questions to determine the approximate time you have for each question.

5) Do not linger over difficult questions

If you come across a difficult question, mark it with a paper clip (useful to have along) and come back to it when you have been through the booklet. One caution if you do this – be sure to skip a number on your answer sheet as well. Check often to be sure that you have not lost your place and that you are marking in the row numbered the same as the question you are answering.

6) Read the questions

Be sure you know what the question asks! Many capable people are unsuccessful because they failed to read the questions correctly.

7) Answer all questions

Unless you have been instructed that a penalty will be deducted for incorrect answers, it is better to guess than to omit a question.

8) Speed tests

It is often better NOT to guess on speed tests. It has been found that on timed tests people are tempted to spend the last few seconds before time is called in marking answers at random – without even reading them – in the hope of picking up a few extra points. To discourage this practice, the instructions may warn you that your score will be "corrected" for guessing. That is, a penalty will be applied. The incorrect answers will be deducted from the correct ones, or some other penalty formula will be used.

9) Review your answers

If you finish before time is called, go back to the questions you guessed or omitted to give them further thought. Review other answers if you have time.

10) Return your test materials

If you are ready to leave before others have finished or time is called, take ALL your materials to the monitor and leave quietly. Never take any test material with you. The monitor can discover whose papers are not complete, and taking a test booklet may be grounds for disqualification.

VIII. EXAMINATION TECHNIQUES

1) Read the general instructions carefully. These are usually printed on the first page of the exam booklet. As a rule, these instructions refer to the timing of the examination; the fact that you should not start work until the signal and must stop work at a signal, etc. If there are any special instructions, such as a choice of questions to be answered, make sure that you note this instruction carefully.

2) When you are ready to start work on the examination, that is as soon as the signal has been given, read the instructions to each question booklet, underline any key words or phrases, such as least, best, outline, describe and the like. In this way you will tend to answer as requested rather than discover on reviewing your paper that you listed without describing, that you selected the worst choice rather than the best choice, etc.

3) If the examination is of the objective or multiple-choice type – that is, each question will also give a series of possible answers: A, B, C or D, and you are called upon to select the best answer and write the letter next to that answer on your answer paper – it is advisable to start answering each question in turn. There may be anywhere from 50 to 100 such questions in the three or four hours allotted and you can see how much time would be taken if you read through all the questions before beginning to answer any. Furthermore, if you

come across a question or group of questions which you know would be difficult to answer, it would undoubtedly affect your handling of all the other questions.

4) If the examination is of the essay type and contains but a few questions, it is a moot point as to whether you should read all the questions before starting to answer any one. Of course, if you are given a choice – say five out of seven and the like – then it is essential to read all the questions so you can eliminate the two that are most difficult. If, however, you are asked to answer all the questions, there may be danger in trying to answer the easiest one first because you may find that you will spend too much time on it. The best technique is to answer the first question, then proceed to the second, etc.

5) Time your answers. Before the exam begins, write down the time it started, then add the time allowed for the examination and write down the time it must be completed, then divide the time available somewhat as follows:
   - If 3-1/2 hours are allowed, that would be 210 minutes. If you have 80 objective-type questions, that would be an average of 2-1/2 minutes per question. Allow yourself no more than 2 minutes per question, or a total of 160 minutes, which will permit about 50 minutes to review.
   - If for the time allotment of 210 minutes there are 7 essay questions to answer, that would average about 30 minutes a question. Give yourself only 25 minutes per question so that you have about 35 minutes to review.

6) The most important instruction is to read each question and make sure you know what is wanted. The second most important instruction is to time yourself properly so that you answer every question. The third most important instruction is to answer every question. Guess if you have to but include something for each question. Remember that you will receive no credit for a blank and will probably receive some credit if you write something in answer to an essay question. If you guess a letter – say "B" for a multiple-choice question – you may have guessed right. If you leave a blank as an answer to a multiple-choice question, the examiners may respect your feelings but it will not add a point to your score. Some exams may penalize you for wrong answers, so in such cases only, you may not want to guess unless you have some basis for your answer.

7) Suggestions
   a. Objective-type questions
      1. Examine the question booklet for proper sequence of pages and questions
      2. Read all instructions carefully
      3. Skip any question which seems too difficult; return to it after all other questions have been answered
      4. Apportion your time properly; do not spend too much time on any single question or group of questions
      5. Note and underline key words – all, most, fewest, least, best, worst, same, opposite, etc.
      6. Pay particular attention to negatives
      7. Note unusual option, e.g., unduly long, short, complex, different or similar in content to the body of the question
      8. Observe the use of "hedging" words – probably, may, most likely, etc.

9. Make sure that your answer is put next to the same number as the question
10. Do not second-guess unless you have good reason to believe the second answer is definitely more correct
11. Cross out original answer if you decide another answer is more accurate; do not erase until you are ready to hand your paper in
12. Answer all questions; guess unless instructed otherwise
13. Leave time for review

b. Essay questions
1. Read each question carefully
2. Determine exactly what is wanted. Underline key words or phrases.
3. Decide on outline or paragraph answer
4. Include many different points and elements unless asked to develop any one or two points or elements
5. Show impartiality by giving pros and cons unless directed to select one side only
6. Make and write down any assumptions you find necessary to answer the questions
7. Watch your English, grammar, punctuation and choice of words
8. Time your answers; don't crowd material

8) Answering the essay question

Most essay questions can be answered by framing the specific response around several key words or ideas. Here are a few such key words or ideas:

M's: manpower, materials, methods, money, management
P's: purpose, program, policy, plan, procedure, practice, problems, pitfalls, personnel, public relations

a. Six basic steps in handling problems:
1. Preliminary plan and background development
2. Collect information, data and facts
3. Analyze and interpret information, data and facts
4. Analyze and develop solutions as well as make recommendations
5. Prepare report and sell recommendations
6. Install recommendations and follow up effectiveness

b. Pitfalls to avoid
1. Taking things for granted – A statement of the situation does not necessarily imply that each of the elements is necessarily true; for example, a complaint may be invalid and biased so that all that can be taken for granted is that a complaint has been registered
2. Considering only one side of a situation – Wherever possible, indicate several alternatives and then point out the reasons you selected the best one
3. Failing to indicate follow up – Whenever your answer indicates action on your part, make certain that you will take proper follow-up action to see how successful your recommendations, procedures or actions turn out to be
4. Taking too long in answering any single question – Remember to time your answers properly

EXAMINATION SECTION

EXAMINATION SECTION
TEST 1

DIRECTIONS: Each question or incomplete statement is followed by several suggested answers or completions. Select the one that BEST answers the question or completes the statement. *PRINT THE LETTER OF THE CORRECT ANSWER IN THE SPACE AT THE RIGHT.*

1. Normal reflexes during the neonatal period include

    A. moro
    B. grasp
    C. stepping
    D. all of the above

2. The milestone MOST likely to occur at 12 weeks of age is the infant's

    A. sustaining social contact
    B. laughing out loud
    C. rolling over
    D. sitting with pelvic support

3. A newborn infant CANNOT

    A. turn his head
    B. touch a surface with his nose
    C. lift his head to the plane of the body
    D. flex around his supporting hand

4. The age at which an infant starts to sustain his head in the plane of the body is APPROXIMATELY _____ month(s).

    A. one   B. two   C. three   D. four

5. At 4 months of age, an infant can do all of the following EXCEPT

    A. sit with a truncal support
    B. show displeasure if social contact is broken
    C. roll over
    D. none of the above

6. An infant starts using pincer movement at APPROXIMATELY _____ of age.

    A. five   B. six   C. eight   D. nine

7. At what age can a child imitate a number or letter figure? _____ months.

    A. 18
    B. 30
    C. 36
    D. None of the above

8. Which of the following is a cognitive milestone achieved by a child at 28 weeks?

    A. Releasing one cube into a cup after demonstration
    B. Raking at a pallet
    C. Uncovering a hidden object
    D. Knowing one or more words and their meanings

9. A 3-month-old infant can do all of the following EXCEPT

    A. listen to music
    B. creep-crawl
    C. fail to grasp
    D. sustain social contact

10. Unassisted pincer movement develops at the age of _____ months. 10.___

    A. four   B. six   C. eight   D. twelve

11. At 6 months of age, developmental milestones do NOT include the child's 11.___

    A. putting a pellet into a bottle
    B. releasing two cubes into a cup
    C. scribbling spontaneously
    D. enjoying a simple ball game

12. Which of the following is NOT a normal accomplishment of a child at 18 months of age? 12.___

    A. Learning to say *no*
    B. Listening to stories while looking at the pictures
    C. Identifying one or more body parts
    D. Kissing parent with a pucker

13. Normal milestones at 2 months of age include the infant's doing each of the following EXCEPT 13.___

    A. reaching at objects
    B. smiling on social contact
    C. attending to voices and coos
    D. following a moving object to 180 visually

14. A 15-month-old child can do all of the following EXCEPT 14.___

    A. walk alone
    B. crawl up stairs
    C. imitate a stroke of crayon
    D. make a tower of 3 cubes

15. During the second year of life, weight gain averages _____ kg per year. 15.___

    A. 1   B. 2.5   C. 3.5   D. 5

16. During the second year of life, height gain averages APPROXIMATELY _____ centimeters per year. 16.___

    A. 2   B. 6   C. 10   D. 15

17. At what age does a child usually reach double the length of his birth length? _____ year(s). 17.___

    A. 1   B. 2   C. 3   D. 4

18. A 15-month-old child can make a tower of _____ cubes. 18.___

    A. 3   B. 5   C. 7   D. 9

19. A 4-year-old child generally CANNOT 19.___

    A. throw a ball   B. climb well
    C. copy a triangle   D. hop on one foot

20. Which of the following is NOT considered a normal motor milestone for a child 3 years of age?

    A. Building a 10-cube tower
    B. Copying a circle
    C. Copying a square
    D. Attempting to draw a person

21. A normally developing 2-year-old child can do all of the following EXCEPT

    A. handle a spoon well
    B. alternate feet while going upstairs
    C. fold paper imitatively
    D. climb on furniture

22. At what age can a child with normal social and cognitive development know his or her own age and sex?
    At _____ months of age.

    A. 18	B. 24	C. 30	D. 36

23. A 3-year-old child can do all of the following EXCEPT

    A. alternate feet while going downstairs
    B. ride a tricycle
    C. hop on one foot
    D. repeat three numbers

24. Nuts, pitted fruits, and popcorn should not be given to a toddler PRIMARILY because they

    A. have almost no food value for a toddler
    B. can cause tooth cavities
    C. will affect the child's appetite
    D. are easily aspirated

25. All of the following statements describe toddlers' well-known sleeping patterns EXCEPT:

    A. Toddlers' sleep needs average 12 hours per day.
    B. A toddler typically discontinues daytime naps around age 3.
    C. A toddler typically sleeps through the night and has at least three daytime naps.
    D. A consistent bedtime ritual helps prepare a toddler for sleep.

26. The one of the following immunizations that is NOT necessary for a toddler to receive is

    A. MMR (measles, mumps, and rubella)
    B. DPT-4, OPV-3 (if not given earlier), PRP-D
    C. HBPV (hemophilus influenzae type B polysaccharide vaccine)
    D. DPT-5, OPV-4

27. Which of the following statements about toddlers' physical growth and development is NOT correct?

    A. Bow-leggedness typically persists through toddlerhood since the legs must bear the weight of the relatively large trunk.
    B. Growth of about 3 inches per year and an average height of 34 inches at age 2 years is normal for toddlers.
    C. Gain of about 4 to 6 lbs. per year and an average weight of 27 lbs. at age 2 years is normal for toddlers.
    D. In toddlers, height and weight increase in a linear fashion.

28. All of the following information about toddlers' psycho-motor milestones is correct EXCEPT:

    A. Sensory changes increase as proximodistal sensations heighten.
    B. The toddler typically begins to walk by age 12 to 15 months, to run by age 2 years, and to walk backward and hop on one foot by age 3 years.
    C. By 24 months of age, a toddler usually achieves fairly good bowel and bladder control.
    D. The toddler usually cannot alternate feet when climbing stairs.

29. All of the following describe normal height and weight changes in children of 3 to 6 years of age EXCEPT:

    A. Gain of 6 to 8 lbs. per year
    B. Average height of 37 inches at age 3, 40 1/2 inches at age 4, and 43 inches at age 5
    C. Growth of 2 1/2 to 3 inches per year
    D. Average weight of 32 lbs. at age 3, 37 lbs. at age 4, and 41 lbs. at age 5

30. Which of the following is NOT a true fact about psycho-motor milestones of children age 3 to 6 years?
    A preschooler

    A. demonstrates increased skill in balancing; by age 4 or 5, he or she can balance on alternate feet with eyes closed
    B. alternates feet when climbing stairs, indicating increased balance and coordination
    C. can successfully perform jobs such as using scissors
    D. is still not skilled enough to tie his or her shoelaces

KEY (CORRECT ANSWERS)

1.	D	16.	B
2.	A	17.	D
3.	C	18.	A
4.	B	19.	C
5.	C	20.	C
6.	D	21.	B
7.	C	22.	D
8.	B	23.	C
9.	B	24.	D
10.	D	25.	C
11.	C	26.	D
12.	B	27.	D
13.	A	28.	C
14.	C	29.	A
15.	B	30.	D

TEST 2

DIRECTIONS: Each question or incomplete statement is followed by several suggested answers or completions. Select the one that BEST answers the question or completes the statement. *PRINT THE LETTER OF THE CORRECT ANSWER IN THE SPACE AT THE RIGHT.*

1. Toys play a useful role in a child's development. All of the following factors should be taken into consideration while selecting a toy for a toddler EXCEPT 1.____

    A. expense
    B. durability
    C. safety
    D. weight

2. All of the following are appropriate and important components for disciplining a toddler EXCEPT 2.____

    A. distraction
    B. admonishment
    C. explanation
    D. praise

3. Which of the following statements MOST accurately describes the toilet training of a toddler? 3.____

    A. Bowel control is accomplished by 18 months.
    B. Daytime bladder control is achieved by 12 to 24 months.
    C. Nightime bladder control is achieved by 24 to 36 months.
    D. Toilet training is usually completed by 4 1/2 years.

4. A toddler's daily nutritional needs from the four basic food groups do NOT include 4.____

    A. two servings from the meat group, 2 tablespoons per serving
    B. four servings from the fruit and vegetable group, 2 tablespoons per serving
    C. seven or more servings of breads and cereals, 1 slice of bread or 3/4 to 1 cup of cereal per serving
    D. 3 cups of milk or milk products

5. John and Peter, both 3 years of age, are fighting over a toy train. 5.____
Which of the following interventions would be the MOST appropriate in this situation?

    A. Admonish them for fighting and tell them to share the train.
    B. Tell them to stop fighting and that there are enough toys to play with, and give Peter puzzles.
    C. Without saying anything, take the train away from the boys and place them in separate parts of the room, giving them some other toys to play with.
    D. Find another train and tell them that they can each have one.

6. Which of the following characteristics is NOT typical of a toddler's language development? 6.____

    A. Begins to use short sentences at 18 months to 2 years
    B. Can remember and repeat 3 numbers by 3 years
    C. Answers questions with multi-word sentences
    D. After knowing own name by 12 months, gives first name by 24 months and full name by 3 years

7. A child commonly experiences more fears during the preschool period than at any other time.
   All of the following are good examples of preschoolers' common fears EXCEPT

   A. being left alone
   B. body mutilation
   C. small animals like rabbits, cats, etc.
   D. objects associated with painful experiences

8. In a conflict situation among preschoolers, which of the following disciplinary principles would be considered the BEST nursing intervention to help the child relieve intensity, regain control, and think about his or her behavior?

   A. Explaining to the child the negative aspects of the conflict
   B. Admonishing the child for the conflict
   C. Distracting the child by providing him with one of the toys he or she likes most
   D. Giving the child a short time-out of 1 minute per year of age

9. All of the following are findings of Freud's theory of psychosexual development of toddlers EXCEPT:

   A. The toddler experiences nothing else but a deep frustration as he or she gains control over containing and releasing bodily waste.
   B. In this stage, the child's focus shifts from the mouth to the anal area, with emphasis on bowel control as he or she gains neuromuscular control over the anal sphincter.
   C. In the *anal stage,* typically extending from age 8 months to 4 years, the erogenous zone is the anus and buttocks, and sexual activity centers on expulsion and retention of bodily waste.
   D. The conflict between *holding on* and *letting go* gradually resolves as bowel training progresses; resolution occurs once control is firmly established.

10. It is NOT true that a toddler of age 15 to 18 months

    A. does not have any signs of temper tantrums yet
    B. walks sideways and backwards
    C. imitates simple things
    D. pulls a toy while walking

11. Which of the following statements about toddlers' play activities is NOT correct?

    A. For a toddler, play is a major socializing medium.
    B. Play typically is parallel - beside rather than with another child.
    C. Push-pull toys help enhance walking skills.
    D. Because of a toddler's long attention span, he or she does not change toys often.

12. Of the following, the INCORRECT statement about toddlers' language and socialization patterns is:

    A. A toddler tends to ask many *what* questions
    B. A toddler typically begins to use longer sentences and has a vocabulary of about 500 words by age 2
    C. A toddler 's social interaction is dominated by ritualism, negativism, and independence

D. Confidence in separating from parents continues to grow

13. Common fears of toddlers include all of the following EXCEPT

    A. loss of parents, separation anxiety
    B. stranger anxiety
    C. musical toys' noises
    D. large animals

14. Discipline strategies are affected by a toddler's temperament. Which of the following disciplinary approaches would likely be the MOST effective for a *difficult* child?

    A. Sustained eye contact and a stern voice
    B. A friendly warning to curtail activities with structured time-out if necessary
    C. Time for gradual introduction to new situations
    D. A quick spanking with explanation for misbehavior

15. The toddler's feeling that commonly develops after a new baby is born, stemming from a sense of *dethronement* since he or she no longer is the sole focus of his parent's attention, is known as

    A. identification   B. mitleiden
    C. sibling rivalry   D. motivation

16. All of the following are considered as important interventions to prevent injuries in toddlers EXCEPT:

    A. Instruct parents to keep crib rails up, place gates across stairways, keep screens secure on all windows, and supervise the toddler at play
    B. Instruct parents never to forget about tightening the car safety belt while riding a toddler around in a car
    C. Teach parents to place all toxic substances up high and locked; secure safety caps on medications; and remove all small, easily aspirated objects from the child's environment
    D. Instruct parents to avoid using table covers to prevent spilling of hot foods or liquids by the child on himself or herself

17. Which of the following statements is NOT part of Piaget's Theory of Cognitive Development of toddlers?

    A. The theory is expressed in two phases, i.e., the Sensorimotor phase and the Preconceptual phase.
    B. The first stage of the Sensorimotor phase explains the primary circular reactions at the age of 12 to 14 months.
    C. The second stage of the Sensorimotor phase explains the beginning of thought at the age of 18 to 24 months, during which time the toddler begins to devise new means for accomplishing tasks through mental calculations.
    D. In the Preconceptual phase, extending from about age 2 to 4 years, the child uses representational thought to recall the past, represent the present, and anticipate the future.

18. According to Kohlberg's Theory of Moral Development of toddlers, moral judgment is a cognitive process that develops gradually at all of these levels EXCEPT the _____ level.

    A. paraconventional
    B. preconventional
    C. conventional
    D. postconventional

19. The Denver Developmental Screening Test (DDST) evaluates a child's _____ development.

    A. social
    B. motor
    C. physical
    D. all of the above

20. According to Erikson's theory of psychosocial development, the toddler begins to master all of the following EXCEPT

    A. individuation
    B. control of bodily functions
    C. control of the sense of autonomy, and moves on to master the task of initiative
    D. acquisition of socially acceptable behavior

21. Kohlberg's Theory of Moral Development for preschoolers does NOT include the finding that

    A. a preschooler is in the preconventional phase of moral development, which extends from 5 to 8 years of age
    B. in this phase, conscience emerges and the emphasis is on external control
    C. a preschooler's preconventional phase of moral development extends from age 4 to 10 years
    D. a preschooler's moral standards are those of others, and he or she observes them either to avoid punishment or to reap rewards

22. Which of the following statements is FALSE concerning the language skills of a preschooler?

    A. A preschooler's vocabulary typically increases to about 1300 words by age 3.
    B. By age 5, a preschooler's vocabulary typically increases to about 2100 words.
    C. A preschooler may talk incessantly and ask many *why* questions.
    D. By age 3, a child usually talks in three- or four-word sentences.

23. Which of the following is considered MOST appropriate to aid gross motor development of a preschooler?

    A. Dress-up clothes
    B. Paints, paper, and crayons
    C. Swimming
    D. Field trips to museums and parks

24. A preschooler needs regular interaction with agemates to help develop _____ skills.

    A. creative
    B. imaginative
    C. motor
    D. social

25. According to Erikson's Theory of Psychosocial Development, between 3 and 6 years of age, a child faces a psycho-social crisis which Erikson terms _____ vs. _____.

    A. definitive; initiative
    B. initiative; terminative
    C. terminative; fear
    D. initiative; guilt

26. According to Erikson's Theory, the development of a sense of guilt occurs when the child is made to feel that his or her imagination and activities are unacceptable.
   Guilt, anxiety, and fear result when the child's thoughts and actions clash with parents'

   A. guilt
   B. fear
   C. anxiety
   D. expectations

27. Freud terms his Theory of Psychosexual Development of Preschoolers all of the following EXCEPT the _____ stage.

   A. phallic
   B. oedipal
   C. oediphallic
   D. all of the above

28. In the phallic stage of Freud's theory, extending from about age 3 to 7, the child's pleasure centers on

   A. the attention given by the parents
   B. friendship with children of the opposite sex
   C. genitalia and masturbation
   D. all of the above

29. Piaget, who defines his Theory of Cognitive Development for preschoolers as a stage of preconceptual thoughts, classifies his theory in two phases, i.e., preconceptual phase and intuitive phase.
   He includes all of the following activities in the preconceptual phase, which extends from age 2 to 4, EXCEPT

   A. making simple classifications
   B. reasoning from specific to specific
   C. exhibiting egocentric thinking
   D. forming concepts that are complete and logical

30. According to the intuitive phase of Piaget's theory, which extends from age 4 to 7, it is NOT correct that a preschooler

   A. becomes capable of classifying, quantifying, and relating objects
   B. exhibits intuitive thought processes
   C. is aware of the principles behind classifying and relating objects
   D. uses many words appropriately but without a real knowledge of their meaning

KEY (CORRECT ANSWERS)

1.	A	16.	B
2.	B	17.	B
3.	A	18.	A
4.	C	19.	D
5.	D	20.	C
6.	C	21.	A
7.	C	22.	A
8.	D	23.	C
9.	A	24.	D
10.	A	25.	D
11.	D	26.	D
12.	B	27.	C
13.	C	28.	C
14.	B	29.	D
15.	C	30.	C

EXAMINATION SECTION
TEST 1

DIRECTIONS: Each question or incomplete statement is followed by several suggested answers or completions. Select the one that BEST answers the question or completes the statement. *PRINT THE LETTER OF THE CORRECT ANSWER IN THE SPACE AT THE RIGHT.*

1. The psychologist whose name is MOST often associated with the theory that the experience of birth has a profound influence on personality development and that an individual who has a slow, prolonged birth is likely to have a personality which fights, struggles and plunges is

   A. Horney
   B. Freud
   C. Sullivan
   D. Rank

2. Which of the following is the MOST correct statement concerning puberty and physical maturity?

   A. Boys and girls who experience early puberty will achieve physical maturity and cease growing later than will the late maturers.
   B. Boys and girls who experience early puberty will achieve physical maturity and cease growing sooner than will the late maturers.
   C. Boys and girls who experience early puberty will achieve physical maturity and cease growing at approximately the same time as the late maturers.
   D. None of the above

3. The MOST prominent difficulties of the middle years of childhood revolve around

   A. relations with peer groups
   B. parent-child relationships
   C. schooling and the ability to learn
   D. physical development

4. In the normal population, the range of achievement of children of the same age in grades 5 and 6 is approximately from

   A. 1 to 2 years
   B. 2 to 4 years
   C. 3 to 5 years
   D. 5 to 8 years

5. The MOST accurate statement concerning anxiety, of the following, is that anxiety is

   A. needed for the socialization process
   B. not needed for the socialization process
   C. less produced by "mental" punishment than by physical punishment
   D. of negligible effect in producing neurosis

6. Of the following, the area of greatest similarity among children is in their

   A. inherited traits
   B. rates of development
   C. sequences of development
   D. patterns of growth dimensions

7. Of the following, which is the MOST significant factor in determining the choice of friends among children between the ages of six and ten?

   A. Mutual interests
   B. Similar personality traits
   C. Conveniently close location
   D. Social and economic standing of parents

8. Lewin, in defining his structural concepts of psychology, represented them

   A. topologically   B. metrically
   C. geometrically   D. orthographically

9. As part of the socialization process, the phenomenon of ambivalence is at its highest intensity during the

   A. toddler years   B. preschool years
   C. early school years   D. intermediate school years

10. The child's need to be a "goody-goody" and his willingness to conform are MOST frequently observed during the

    A. phallic period   B. latency period
    C. prepubertal period   D. adolescent period

11. Joe Flirp is a great health education teacher, to a large extent, because the boys model themselves after him. The foregoing illustrates the psychological mechanism of

    A. sublimation   B. displacement
    C. regression   D. identification

12. "You're much too authoritarian," said the principal to the teacher. "And I won't stand for that in my school." The principal is demonstrating the psychological mechanism of

    A. sublimation   B. conversion
    C. projection   D. identification

13. Margaret Snorble, unhappy because of her lack of friendship, devoted all her energy to studying. She became the number one student in her grade. Margaret is demonstrating the psychological mechanism of

    A. sublimation   B. conversion
    C. introjection   D. fantasy

14. Ben was ill now and then. However, each time after a short rest, he quickly became well. This tendency or process is known as

    A. redintegration   B. regression
    C. homeostasis   D. somatistation

15. Joanie asked for apple pie and was told that there was none left. "Oh, well," said she, "give me peach pie. I like it better anyway." Joanie is demonstrating the psychological mechanism of

    A. regression   B. displacement
    C. rationalization   D. sublimation

16. The principal had just left after telling Miss Jones she had to improve the quality of her lesson plans. Tears came to her eyes; she stamped her foot several times, pounded on the desk and then broke into uncontrolled sobbing. Miss Jones' behavior is an example of the psychological mechanism of

    A. introjection
    B. projection
    C. sublimation
    D. regression

17. Of the following statements concerning praise and punishment, which is LEAST in accord with modern psychological principles?

    A. When a child is bad, spank him.
    B. When a child is bad, say, "If you're not good, I won't love you any more."
    C. When a child is good, give him something to show your approval.
    D. When a child is good, say, "That's O.K. Let's try to do better next time."

18. Which one of the following is NOT characteristic of the development of a group?

    A. Emergence of collective goals
    B. Solidification of individual roles within the group structure
    C. Growth of group norms for behavior
    D. Development of a group atmosphere or social climate

19. The status of an individual in a group is determined, for the MOST part, by

    A. the possession of those qualities the group deems important
    B. his socio-economic level
    C. his status in other groups of which he is a member
    D. the amount of time and energy he is willing to devote to the purposes of the group

20. In comparison with other members of a group, the leader tends to

    A. hold himself in higher esteem
    B. be less spontaneous
    C. be more desirous of being of service to others
    D. be more willing to accept a low level of performance from members of the group

21. The individual who emerges as the leader of a group is usually

    A. the person who, in the judgment of the group, can best meet the demands of the particular problem
    B. superior to the other members of the group in a wide variety of abilities
    C. chosen on the basis of personal qualities rather than ability
    D. the same person, no matter in what activities the group participates

22. The degree of cohesiveness which has been established in a group is MOST likely to be lowered by

    A. unfavorable evaluation of the group by outsiders
    B. favorable evaluation of the group by outsiders
    C. decreasing the amount of interaction in the group
    D. increasing the degree of interaction in the group

23. Research has shown that neighborhood gangs tend to be more cohesive than groups of the same age functioning as clubs in more formal youth agencies. This would suggest that

    A. the club is potentially longer-lived than the gang
    B. young people join clubs only if they are not accepted by the gang
    C. clubs will not be able to function adequately in a given neighborhood until some way is found to destroy gangs already in existence
    D. the activities of the gang meet the needs of its members better than those of the club program do

24. Studies of the cohesiveness of small groups have indicated that the more cohesive a group, the

    A. more willing will the group be to defend itself against external criticism
    B. less likely is it that the group will permit internal disagreement with its objective or goals
    C. less perceptive is the group of its own solidarity
    D. more susceptible is the group to disruption caused by loss of a leader

25. According to Sullivan, anxiety serves as a defense against the danger of

    A. conditioned fears
    B. self-discovery
    C. destructive people on the outside
    D. interpersonal destructiveness

26. The system of classifying people into those who move towards, against, and away from people was devised by

    A. Alexander   B. Fromm
    C. Fenichel   D. Horney

27. Scientific investigators generally agree that the development of human behavior begins

    A. at the time of conception
    B. during the prenatal period
    C. at birth
    D. at the time of initial social interaction

28. Of the following, the MOST frequent reason why two 11-year old boys stop "being friends" is

    A. lack of agreement concerning activities to be undertaken
    B. lack of recent contact
    C. a clash of personalities
    D. parental disapproval

29. Of the following, the MOST important determinant of leadership in pre-adolescent children is the child's

    A. self-confidence   B. sex
    C. physical attractiveness D. socio-economic status

30. Of the following, the one MOST likely to be associated with poor emotional development in a sixth-grade girl is

   A. lack of interest in boys
   B. striving for perfection in all her school work
   C. desire to please her parents in everything she does
   D. a strong interest in arithmetic, with only passive interest in other school subjects

31. The author of FOUNDATIONS OF READING INSTRUCTION is

   A. Paul Witty
   B. Emmett A. Betts
   C. David H. Russell
   D. Helen M. Robinson

32. The Dolch 220-word basic vocabulary consists of words that

   A. are most commonly used in fifteen basic readers on first and second grade levels
   B. are most commonly used in compositions by primary-grade children
   C. must be recognized as "sight words" because they do not follow regular phonetic principles
   D. make up fifty percent of reading matter used in the elementary schools

33. The MOST rapid rate of growth among children between the ages of 2 and 8 is found at age

   A. 2   B. 4   C. 6   D. 8

34. Studies of the relationship between sex and reading disability of elementary school pupils generally reveal that among pupils with reading disabilities the number of

   A. girls exceeds the number of boys
   B. boys and girls is about equal
   C. boys is slightly greater than the number of girls
   D. boys is about 3 times the number of girls

35. Research reports agree that the reading interests of groups of children

   A. begin to be different for boys and girls during the primary grades
   B. change consistently as children grow older
   C. center on animal stories during pre-adolescent years
   D. show no difference between boys and girls until junion high school years

36. The MOST accurate statement to make regarding the cause of reading disability is that research shows that most reading difficulties are primarily due to

   A. low intelligence
   B. familial discord
   C. insufficient motivation to read
   D. a complex of interrelated factors

37. Fernald's name is associated with a teaching procedure by which a child learns words by means of a

   A. look-and-say technique
   B. visual motor approach
   C. tracing-and-writing procedure
   D. letter sound blending approach

38. A diagnostic report of a child's reading states that he has no word analysis techniques. This diagnosis is equivalent to saying that he

    A. has a poor meaningful vocabulary
    B. cannot understand what he reads
    C. cannot sound out words
    D. cannot adjust his rate

39. Where mixed dominance is identified as a possible causal factor for a child who makes many reversal errors, it would be BEST for the teacher to

    A. stress left to right direction in reading
    B. change the child's hand preference
    C. change the child's eye preference
    D. stress an oral approach in reading

40. The mother of a first-grade child is concerned about her child's reading. It appears that the child can read only the words in her primer, but cannot sound out any words not in her book. Of the following, the BEST explanation to the mother would be that

    A. it is all right because the children are not taught phonics today
    B. it is all right because the child will learn to sound words
    C. it is serious and the child will get special help soon
    D. it is all right since children are taught to read whole words first, then the sounds

41. As a means of changing the current behavior pattern of an adolescent, which of the following forces will generally prove to be MOST potent? Disapproval of the behavior pattern by

    A. the adolescent's parents
    B. his classroom teacher
    C. a group of his peers
    D. an adult he admires

42. Of the following, the characteristic that is MOST important in determining an individual's status in a group of pre-adolescent girls is her

    A. school achievement   B. socio-economic status
    C. ability to make friends   D. intelligence

43. If the results of studies of boys' clubs are applicable to the school situation, one may expect the greatest amount of aggressive behavior to be noted in classes where the classroom climate may be described as

    A. permissive   B. laissez-faire
    C. democratic   D. autocratic

44. Which of the following authors would you be LEAST likely to recommend for information about child care?

    A. Sidonie Gruenberg   B. Jean Piaget
    C. Ernest Harms   D. Benjamin Spock

45. Of the following, which one is NOT an authority in reading? 45._____

    A. Gates   B. Russell
    C. Harris   D. Bullis

46. Studies have shown that the ratio of reading disability among boys as compared to girls is: 46._____

    A. 4 to 1   B. 3 to 1   C. 2 to 1   D. equal

47. Which of the following terms refers to the maintenance of stability in the physiological functioning of the organism? 47._____

    A. functional autonomy   B. canalization
    C. homeostasis   D. maturation

48. A recent comprehensive survey of child-rearing patterns in America found mothers of the working class when compared in their toilet-training practices with mothers of the middle class to be 48._____

    A. more permissive   B. more indifferent
    C. more severe   D. more accepting

49. Studies of the relationship of body build and character traits have in general been found to be 49._____

    A. positively correlated
    B. negatively correlated
    C. statistically significantly correlated
    D. inconclusive

50. The theory that psychical compensation for a feeling of physical or social inferiority is responsible for the development of a psychoneurosis is attributed to 50._____

    A. Adler   B. Horney
    C. Freud   D. Sullivan

KEY (CORRECT ANSWERS)

1. D	11. D	21. A	31. B	41. C
2. B	12. C	22. C	32. D	42. C
3. C	13. A	23. D	33. A	43. D
4. D	14. C	24. A	34. D	44. B
5. A	15. C	25. B	35. B	45. D
6. C	16. D	26. D	36. D	46. B
7. C	17. B	27. B	37. C	47. C
8. A	18. B	28. B	38. C	48. C
9. B	19. A	29. A	39. A	49. D
10. B	20. A	30. B	40. D	50. A

TEST 2

DIRECTIONS: Each question or incomplete statement is followed by several suggested answers or completions. Select the one that BEST answers the question or completes the statement. *PRINT THE LETTER OF THE CORRECT ANSWER IN THE SPACE AT THE RIGHT.*

1. Of the following, the MOST important consideration in distinguishing anxiety from fear is the

    A. intensity of the emotion
    B. extent of relation to subjective as distinguished from objective conditions
    C. actuality of danger
    D. strength of the personality organization of the one who is affected

    1.____

2. Wishes of children of elementary school age deal mainly with

    A. improvement of their own inner strength, character, or intelligence
    B. improvement of their personal appearance
    C. possessions, pleasant experiences, privileges, opportunities for enjoyment
    D. exploitation of family relationships

    2.____

3. The psychological climate of the home which influences adjustment of the child is MOST closely related to the

    A. number of children in the home
    B. educational level of the parents
    C. occupational level of the father
    D. attitudes of the parents

    3.____

4. With reference to emotional stability, intellectually gifted children as a group compared to average children are

    A. generally inferior   B. the same
    C. generally superior   D. unpredictably related

    4.____

5. Piaget distinguishes between two kinds of thought, logical and autistic. It is his thesis that the child's way of thinking is

    A. basically autistic
    B. either logical or autistic
    C. basically logical
    D. situated between the logical and the autistic

    5.____

6. According to research findings, the MOST effective way to help a child deal with a specific fear, such as a fear of dogs, is to

    A. have the parents and others who are close to the child set an example of fearlessness
    B. explain matters to him in terms he can understand readily
    C. help him by degrees to come actively and directly to grips with the situation
    D. try to effect "positive reconditioning" by presenting the feared stimulus with an attractive one

    6.____

7. A fundamental principle of the psychoanalytic school which has been accepted by most schools of psychology is the

   A. development of the collective unconscious
   B. theory of the existence of a dynamic unconscious
   C. development of an oedipus complex situation
   D. relationship between early psychosexual development and later adult behavior

8. In comparing the rate of biological growth for boys and girls between the ages of 5-7 and 7-10, the latter period shows

   A. a slightly more accelerated rate than the former
   B. a slightly less accelerated rate than the former
   C. a markedly more accelerated rate than the former
   D. a rate equal to the former period

9. The concept of "stages" in describing human development is LEAST applicable to

   A. Freud's psychoanalytic theory
   B. Piaget's cognitive theory
   C. Skinner's behavior theory
   D. Erikson's personality theory

10. The principal effect of nursery school attendance is upon the child's

    A. social development
    B. intellectual development
    C. perceptual development
    D. motor development

11. Which of the following terms is MOST clearly associated with stubborn reading disability?

    A. Apraxia   B. Dysplasia   C. Dyslexia   D. Aphasia

12. The boy who is encouraged or required to be more independent at an earlier age tends to develop a(n)

    A. low threshold for frustration
    B. inability to work well with others
    C. reluctance to accept adult authority
    D. strong need to achieve

13. Pioneering studies in eliminating children's fears were conducted by Mary Cover Jones. The methods used, which are consistent with present-day learning theory, included all but ONE of the following:

    A. Direct conditioning
    B. Social imitation
    C. Feeding responses
    D. Systematic desensitization

14. In contrast to upward mobile adolescents, downward mobile adolescents are

    A. less ambivalent in self-concept
    B. less interested in job security
    C. more confident in social relationships
    D. more dependent on their parents

15. In which of the following situations would a classroom atmosphere of competitiveness be LEAST detrimental to the cultivation of interpersonal relationships? Classmates are

    A. unfamiliar with one another, but equal in abilities
    B. familiar with one another and equal in abilities
    C. unfamiliar with one another and greatly disparate in abilities
    D. familiar with one another and greatly disparate in abilities

16. On group intelligence tests, Cyril Burt found the highest correlations between

    A. identical twins reared apart
    B. siblings reared together
    C. parents and own children living together
    D. identical twins reared together

17. An adolescent boy would like to have a girlfriend. As an example of sublimation, he might

    A. proclaim himself a "woman-hater"
    B. withdraw from all interpersonal relationships
    C. convince himself that girls are really crazy about him
    D. begin to write romantic poetry

18. Jim studies all night before an examination in an attempt to learn the entire course. This is an example of

    A. distributed practice   B. massed practice
    C. practice effect   D. spread of effect

19. The best-controlled studies of the influence of genetic factors on human behavior are found in investigations of

    A. newborn babies   B. identical twins
    C. fraternal twins   D. siblings

20. Terman's follow-up studies on a group of gifted children as compared to children of average intelligence revealed them to have

    A. better adjustment as shown on personality and character tests
    B. greater physical problems
    C. lower incomes
    D. more uneven academic achievement

21. Which one of the following is the MOST important determinant of leadership among pre-adolescent boys?

    A. Intellectual ability
    B. Physical size and strength
    C. Popularity with girls
    D. Sensitivity to the needs of others

22. Billy wants to be admired, but he is too clumsy to achieve this goal through sports. Therefore, although not a bright pupil, he studies long hours and earns very high grades. This may be cited as an example of

    A. compensation
    B. projection
    C. rationalization
    D. reaction formation

23. Of the following, the MOST important factor making for the development of friendship among young children is

    A. similarity in interests
    B. similarity in social class
    C. geographic proximity
    D. friendship among parents

24. Harlow's work on mothering in monkeys suggests that the affective bond between the infant and the mother is based on

    A. feeding
    B. grooming
    C. tactile contact
    D. primitive vocalization

25. The CORRECT order of Piaget's developmental stages is

    A. concrete operations, preoperational, sensorimotor, formal operational
    B. concrete operations, sensorimotor, preoperational, formal operational
    C. sensorimotor, concrete operations, preoperational, formal operational
    D. sensorimotor, preoperational, concrete operations, formal operational

26. Piaget's process which states that children invent increasingly more and better schemata for adapting to their environment is known as

    A. assimilation
    B. equilibrium
    C. accommodation
    D. conservation

27. Which of the following is NOT considered by Erikson to be a developmental task of adolescence?

    A. Development of a sense of shared identity with another
    B. Development of sexual identity
    C. Ability to see one's life in perspective
    D. Experimentation with different roles

28. A six-year-old child who is able to solve a conservation problem would be classified under which of the following stages described by Piaget?

    A. Sensorimotor
    B. Formal operations
    C. Preoperational
    D. Concrete operations

29. During adolescence, girls *generally* surpass boys in

    A. scientific ability
    B. mathematical ability
    C. ability to perform verbal tasks
    D. gross motor skills

30. The CORRECT order of Freud's stages of psychosexual development is:

    A. Oral, latency, anal, phallic, genital
    B. Oral, anal, phallic, latency, genital
    C. Phallic, oral, anal, latency, genital
    D. Latency, oral, genital, anal, phallic

31. According to Erikson, a MAJOR developmental conflict a child faces in the elementary school age period is the conflict between

    A. initiative and guilt
    B. identity and identity diffusion
    C. industry and inferiority
    D. trust and mistrust

32. According to Piaget, in the preoperational stage children

    A. begin to classify and order activities internally
    B. begin to integrate sensory and motor activities
    C. gain the ability to think logically about a problem
    D. are unable to transcend the here and now and are dependent on immediate perception

33. A pupil is able to reason simultaneously about whole and part and is able to classify according to two or three properties. According to Piaget, the pupil is in the _____ stage.

    A. sensory-motor
    B. formal operations
    C. preoperational
    D. concrete operations

34. According to Kohlberg, moral development proceeds through a sequence of stages that are

    A. dependent on the individual's personality and the way in which society reacts to that personality
    B. strongly influenced by individual differences in educational experience and religious training
    C. characterized by increasing symmetry, conventionality, and objectivity
    D. universal and invariant from one culture to another

35. The technique in which a particular form or sequence of behavior is established by reinforcing successively closer approximations to that behavior is called

    A. discriminative responding
    B. shaping
    C. classical conditioning
    D. fading

36. The HIGHEST need in Maslow's hierarchy of human needs is

    A. safety
    B. love
    C. self-actualization
    D. integration

37. According to Piaget, a child's thinking becomes completely general and capable of dealing with the hypothetical during the _____ stage.

    A. sensorimotor
    B. concrete operations
    C. preoperational
    D. formal operations

38. MOST child development specialists believe that a child's peer groups begin to replace the family as a socializing agent

    A. after the age of 5 or 6
    B. between the age of 2 or 3
    C. near the beginning of adolescence
    D. toward the end of adolescence

39. According to Erik Erikson, a key developmental task for the early elementary school years involves

    A. establishing a personal identity
    B. building confidence, resourcefulness, and enthusiasm
    C. surviving a psychosocial moratorium
    D. handling developmental discontinuity

40. Peter maintains that "everyone else in my class thinks I'm a crook." The mechanism of adjustment Peter is probably utilizing is usually referred to as

    A. projection
    B. rationalization
    C. compensation
    D. identification

41. Of the following, the BEST means of helping a child develop tolerance for tension is to

    A. protect the child from experiencing frustration
    B. make the child face reality through frequent experience of failure
    C. make sure that the child is uniformly successful
    D. help the child achieve some success and face some failure

42. Phil always develops a headache when he is called upon to complete a difficult task. Phil's headache is a(n)

    A. hysteroid reaction
    B. compensatory reaction
    C. reaction formation
    D. paranoid reaction

43. Which of the following is characteristic of the person who overcompensates?

    A. Projection
    B. Repression
    C. Self-repudiation
    D. Rationalization

44. A child who has been rejected by his parents tries to "show off" at every opportunity. Such a child is usually

    A. unaware of the nature of his frustration
    B. not capable of reacting more effectively
    C. reacting objectively to his stress situation
    D. deliberately trying to show his parents his need for affection

45. CHILD-CENTERED GROUP GUIDANCE OF PARENTS as described by Slavson deals with

    A. the understanding of the behavior and specific acts
    B. of children and ways of dealing with them appropriately
    C. free-associative catharsis which uncovers anxiety-inducing memories, acts and situations
    D. diminution of guilt on the part of the parents
    E. intellectually recognizing and emotionally accepting latent, covert and repressed impulses and strivings in children

46. Which of the following statements BEST expresses the central theme in Bruno Bettelheim's book, LOVE IS NOT ENOUGH? The disturbed child needs to identify with a person who

    A. accepts his feelings
    B. clearly structures his environment
    C. permits regression
    D. is maternal and "giving"

47. The leisure time activities of the typical pre-adolescent boys' group are mainly given over to

    A. a succession of activities suited to a changing number of players
    B. games governed by a highly organized series of rules
    C. aimless circulation over a relatively large area looking for something to do
    D. just "hanging around with the boys"

48. The normal age range of reading ability between the best and the poorest reader in a typical sixth grade is about

    A. 2 years   B. 3 years
    C. 5 years   D. 7 years

49. Of the following books, the one NOT written by A.T. Jersild is

    A. IN SEARCH OF SELF
    B. CHILDREN'S FEARS
    C. LOVE IS NOT ENOUGH
    D. WHEN TEACHERS FACE THEMSELVES

50. Studies in child development at Yale University were done primarily under the direction of

    A. Lawrence K. Frank   B. Samuel R. Slavson
    C. Arnold Gesell   D. Albert Deutsch

KEY (CORRECT ANSWERS)

1. B	11. C	21. B	31. C	41. D
2. C	12. D	22. A	32. A	42. A
3. D	13. D	23. C	33. B	43. C
4. C	14. D	24. C	34. B	44. A
5. D	15. B	25. D	35. B	45. A
6. C	16. D	26. B	36. C	46. A
7. B	17. D	27. C	37. D	47. A
8. B	18. B	28. D	38. D	48. D
9. C	19. B	29. C	39. A	49. C
10. A	20. A	30. B	40. A	50. C

EXAMINATION SECTION
TEST 1

DIRECTIONS: Each question or incomplete statement is followed by several suggested answers or completions. Select the one that BEST answers the question or completes the statement. *PRINT THE LETTER OF THE CORRECT ANSWER IN THE SPACE AT THE RIGHT.*

1. The peer group serves the individual in the socialization process by

   A. showing him how to relate to other groups
   B. showing him how to be mature
   C. helping him to achieve an identity for himself
   D. helping him accept the discipline of his family

2. The age at which intelligence tests yield the MOST reliable prediction of future academic performance is

   A. 2-4   B. 4-6   C. 6-8   D. 12-14

3. Many studies have explored the effects of maternal deprivation on children. The findings indicate that such deprived children are MOST likely to be

   A. independent and active
   B. inert, withdrawn, mentally retarded and physically inferior
   C. less prone to infectious diseases because there is less danger of infection from others
   D. socially responsive to other adults

4. Of the following, which is MOST characteristic of the late maturing adolescent boy?

   A. Better adjustment to his age mates
   B. Greater independence of others
   C. Better acceptance of discipline
   D. Consistently negative evaluation of himself

5. Of the following, the major cause of juvenile delinquency is

   A. parental rejection   B. poverty
   C. culture conflict   D. inferior biological structure

6. In the recent research and study concerning the learning of disadvantaged youth, the MOST important single finding has been that

   A. the pre-school is the level of education which must be expanded
   B. the mother is the key factor in the enrichment of the socially disadvantaged
   C. the model the child identifies with must be well chosen
   D. little can be done for delinquent girls after seventeen years of age

7. An author who concerns himself with the "epigenetic principle of gradual unfoldings," the principle that the successive differentiations made during a lifetime provide a person with a developmental concept of self, is

   A. Esther Lloyd-Jones   B. Erik Erikson
   C. John Dewey   D. Edmund G. Williamson

8. The belief that power and status motives are MORE significant for behavior than broadly sexual motives was advocated by

   A. Freud
   B. Adler
   C. Jung
   D. Rank

9. Of all children, what percentage is generally considered to be mentally retarded?

   A. .5 B. 3.0 C. 10.0 D. 15.0

10. Studies of social acceptance show that gifted children are

    A. less socially acceptable than the average
    B. more socially acceptable than the retarded but less socially acceptable than the average
    C. more socially acceptable than the average and far more than the retarded
    D. no more socially accepted than the average

11. Of the following, the major characteristic of autistic type schizophrenic children is

    A. psychosomatic symptoms
    B. extreme withdrawal tendencies
    C. psychopathic symptoms
    D. extreme suspiciousness of adults

12. Of the following, the protective test MOST useful in studying the body-image of crippled children is the

    A. CHILDREN'S APPERCEPTION TEST
    B. BLACKY TEST
    C. MACHOVER DRAW-A-PERSON
    D. HOUSE-TREE-PERSON

13. The MOST serious problem for the cerebral palsied which contributes to learning difficulty in school, next to speech, is

    A. defective vision
    B. left-handedness
    C. hearing
    D. hand and eye coordination

14. Of the following symptoms, which is MOST characteristic of brain damaged children?

    A. Perseveration
    B. Echolalia
    C. Hallucinations
    D. Anorexia

15. Of the following, the organization that would be MOST helpful in working with a child suffering from athetosis would be the

    A. Association for the Help of Retarded Children
    B. United Cerebral Palsy Association
    C. Parents' Association for CRMD
    D. League for Epilepsy

16. The behavior patterns that develop during adolescence are

    A. genetically determined
    B. culturally determined
    C. physiologically determined
    D. found in all societies

17. According to Erikson, if a child has his needs thoroughly satisfied during his childhood, he is *most likely* to be an adolescent who is

    A. over-demanding
    B. unable to meet frustration
    C. over-achieving
    D. successful in personal-social development

18. Research evidence on girls' fears indicates that their fears during the oepidal period involve the type of anxiety known as

    A. separation
    B. fixation
    C. castration
    D. deprivation

19. In the University of Chicago study on identical twins reared apart, the GREATEST similarity found was in

    A. intelligence
    B. vocational choice
    C. personality
    D. physical appearance

20. In which of the following groups of adolescents are personal problems in adjustment MOST likely to arise?

    A. Early maturing boys and girls
    B. Late maturing boys and girls
    C. Early maturing girls and late maturing boys
    D. Late maturing girls and early maturing boys

21. The adolescent gang structure fulfills the unsatisfied needs of lower class youth through his acquisition of

    A. social skills
    B. intellectual and vocational interests
    C. athletic skills
    D. sanctions for his own aggression

22. The major limitation of the sociogram and sociometric test is that it does NOT disclose the

    A. status of the individual
    B. variety of choice
    C. organization pattern
    D. factors underlying choice

23. In establishing identity and sex role, the adolescent is MOST likely to be influenced by which of the following?

    A. Parents
    B. Siblings
    C. Peers
    D. Teachers

24. Studies on the characteristics of intellectually dull adolescents indicate

    A. inferior physical development on the part of the dull as compared with normal children
    B. more frequent eye, ear and speech defects among the dull children
    C. no clear social or emotional difference between dull and normal children
    D. all of the above characteristics to be true

25. "I made the varsity basketball and football teams but the coach cut me off the track squad." This statement embodies which of the following ego-defense mechanisms?

    A. Projection   B. Sublimation
    C. Repression   D. Regression

26. Considering the various informal groups which exist in a school system, such as faculty friendship groups, student clubs, cliques, and gangs, it is noticeable that the members of each group tend to possess common information and common ideas in many respects. These group beliefs exist because

    A. of the initial self-selection of the group by its members
    B. information is filtered through group leaders
    C. members are subjected to the same range of information
    D. all of the above are true

27. Of the following, the information that a sociogram does NOT reveal is the

    A. general pattern of group organization
    B. network of group communication
    C. reasons for choices and rejections
    D. relative strength of choice status of individual members

28. The weaknesses in cross-sectional studies of adolescents lie in the fact that

    A. only those who survive through the high school are sampled
    B. only the lower levels of the socio-economic groups are sampled
    C. only some interrelationships of the aspects of growth are studied
    D. the lower levels of ability are also sampled

29. The stimulus-response theory of learning explains behavior in terms of

    A. subliminal motivational cues
    B. heredity and environment
    C. physiological processes
    D. learning by insight

30. Of the following, the major weakness of a sociometric test of social acceptability that asks only for positive choices is that it

    A. has a bad mental hygiene effect on the class
    B. crystallizes the groups' opinions of each other
    C. will give a good picture of the children in the middle range of acceptability
    D. fails to distinguish between the "overlooked" children and those who are rejected

31. In "Jonesville," middle class adolescents asked to name their best friends usually chose someone

    A. of their own social class
    B. of higher status than their own
    C. below them in social status
    D. they liked for personal reasons; their choices were distributed among all social classes

32. A common change in the personality defenses of the adolescent child is the development of

    A. greater intellectualism and isolation of affect
    B. a tendency toward avoidance and denial
    C. suspicion and withdrawal
    D. repression and literal-mindedness

33. Studies on the development of sex characteristics during pubescent growth indicate that

    A. the sequence in the development of sex characteristics is marked by great consistency
    B. the age at which specific sex characteristics appear is quite reliable
    C. the only differences in the age occurrence of specific characteristics is due to sex differences
    D. there is little range in size or variability of sex characteristics

34. Adler, Horney, and Rank are deviationists from which one of the following theories?

    A. Psychoanalytical
    B. Rogerian
    C. Communications
    D. Neobehavioral

35. All of the following are identified with behavioral counseling EXCEPT

    A. Williamson
    B. Skinner
    C. Eysenck
    D. Krumboltz

36. All of the following associations are correct EXCEPT

    A. endomorphy - softness and spherical appearance
    B. mesomorphy - hard and rectangular physique with a predominance of bone and muscle
    C. ectomorphy - a linear and fragile physique
    D. gynandromorphy - a physique that represents an exaggeration of sexual characteristics associated with the given sex

37. Psychiatrists generally agree that the three characteristics *usually* combined in a severely troubled child are

    A. laziness, hostility, withdrawal
    B. slight height, overweight, pallor
    C. lack of relatedness, a speech problem, an eating problem
    D. undernourishment, fatigue, lack of coordination

38. Directing an emotion toward a safe or acceptable object as a substitute for a dangerous or unacceptable object is a fairly good definition for which one of the following defense mechanisms?

    A. Displacement
    B. Repression
    C. Identification
    D. Rationalization

39. The "latency period" as a concept of psychoanalysis has reference to the

    A. years between early childhood and adolescence
    B. period during which successful toilet training (accommodation to time, place and manner) is normally achieved
    C. period during which the oedipal strivings reach their peak
    D. period of pubertal development

40. An unpopular girl frequently calls attention to the social deficiencies in others. Her behavior illustrates

    A. regression
    B. projection
    C. repression
    D. rationalization

41. Which one of the following was NOT supported by Kurt Lewin's research?

    A. People are more apt to change if they participate in a decision to change.
    B. It is easier to change individuals in a group situation rather than singly.
    C. Change brought about through groups was more lasting than that brought about singly.
    D. While pressures of group members upon individuals were very strong, they were not as influential as those of group leaders.

42. A six-year-old child should normally be expected to do all of the following EXCEPT

    A. play simple games
    B. put on a sweater without help
    C. draw with a crayon
    D. write in sentences

43. An educational television program developed especially for pre-school age children is

    A. Learning Your A B C's
    B. Sesame Street
    C. The Number Game
    D. The Partridge Family

44. Which of the following statements concerning masturbation in children is NOT true?

    A. Excessive masturbation can injure a child's genitals.
    B. Masturbation is practiced by most children at some point of their development.
    C. Masturbation may be a symptom of tenseness and nervousness in a child.
    D. There tends to be an increased urge to masturbate during adolescence.

45. A child's rate of physical growth is MOST rapid during the period

    A. from birth to two years
    B. from six to nine years
    C. of pre-adolescence
    D. of adolescence

46. In planning activities for a group of ten-year-old children, the children's counselor should   46._____

    A. encourage the children to participate in the planning
    B. schedule activities that are the easiest to plan
    C. realize that children at this age like to watch television
    D. insist that each child participate in each activity

47. A child of twelve would be MOST likely to find an outlet for his aggressive tendencies in   47._____

    A. watching television
    B. participating in athletics
    C. reading a history book
    D. playing checkers

48. Of the following, the statement which MOST accurately describes the physical development of boys and girls during adolescence is that   48._____

    A. girls generally mature earlier than boys
    B. boys generally mature earlier than girls
    C. boys and girls generally mature at about the same age
    D. physically active boys and girls generally mature earlier than physically inactive ones

49. The average child has not developed all the many abilities needed for beginning reading until the age of about   49._____

    A. two   B. four   C. six   D. eight

50. Which of the following situations indicates that the child is probably emotionally disturbed?   50._____

    A. A five-year-old girl suddenly starts behaving like a baby after the birth of her sister.
    B. A four-year-old boy keeps asking for his father, although he has been told repeatedly that his father has died.
    C. A ten-year-old boy has refused to play with other children since he first entered school five years ago.
    D. All of the above

KEY (CORRECT ANSWERS)

1. C	11. B	21. D	31. B	41. D
2. C	12. C	22. D	32. A	42. D
3. B	13. D	23. C	33. A	43. B
4. D	14. A	24. D	34. A	44. A
5. A	15. B	25. A	35. A	45. A
6. A	16. B	26. D	36. D	46. A
7. B	17. D	27. C	37. C	47. B
8. B	18. C	28. A	38. A	48. A
9. B	19. D	29. C	39. A	49. C
10. C	20. C	30. D	40. B	50. C

TEST 2

DIRECTIONS: Each question or incomplete statement is followed by several suggested answers or completions. Select the one that BEST answers the question or completes the statement. *PRINT THE LETTER OF THE CORRECT ANSWER IN THE SPACE AT THE RIGHT.*

1. The process by which children take to themselves the values, the thinking, and social behavior of their parents is called

    A. projection
    B. identification
    C. fixation
    D. sublimation

    1.____

2. Of the following, the characteristic that MOST clearly differentiates primary drives from secondary drives is that primary drives

    A. are related to biological needs that must be satisfied
    B. are learned early in the developmental cycle
    C. are derived from complex patterns of behavior
    D. may be observed after biological needs have been met

    2.____

3. Spitz and Goldfarb, in two different studies, have suggested that children who will have predictably lower I.Q's are those reared in

    A. institutions
    B. broken homes
    C. foster homes
    D. middle class homes

    3.____

4. One of the MOST common fears of early childhood is the fear of

    A. animals
    B. being separated from parents
    C. being rejected by peers
    D. having too much independence

    4.____

5. The average child shows the FIRST signs of laughing responses

    A. before the age of six months
    B. between the ages of six months and one year
    C. at the age of about one year
    D. at the age of about fifteen months

    5.____

6. A child is LEAST likely to choose a child of the opposite sex to play with at the age of

    A. two
    B. four
    C. seven
    D. ten

    6.____

7. When toilet training a two-year-old child, the children's counselor should

    A. scold the child when she wets her pants
    B. take the child to the bathroom only when she asks to go
    C. have the child sit on the toilet for long periods of time
    D. keep the toilet training routine free from tension

    7.____

8. The average child of three years MOST often shows his anger by

   A. breaking things
   B. crying
   C. threatening his mother
   D. sulking

9. Children at the age of two or three occasionally have temper tantrums when they do not get what they want. Of the following, the BEST method for a children's counselor to use when faced with a temper tantrum by a two-year-old child in her group is to

   A. allow the child to have what he wants
   B. try to reason with the child by explaining why he cannot have what he wants
   C. wait until the worst of the temper tantrum is over and then make a friendly gesture toward the child
   D. order the child to stop this behavior

10. All of the following are good principles to follow in administering punishment to a three-year-old child EXCEPT the

    A. punishment should be administered immediately after the incident of bad behavior
    B. child should be punished only if he understands why his behavior was bad
    C. specific punishment should be appropriate to the specific case of bad behavior
    D. punishment should be administered in an impartial manner

11. Helen, a 14-year-old girl, has two younger sisters who are more successful than she in school. Her mother complains that at home Helen constantly makes remarks intended to hurt their feelings. Helen's behavior is BEST characterized as a form of

    A. compulsion   B. sublimation
    C. rationalization   D. projection

12. Overlearning is primarily an outgrowth of

    A. removal of inhibitions   B. additional practice
    C. strong motivation   D. fear of failure

13. "The mind responds to relationships, not to fixed stimuli" is associated with the movement in psychology known as

    A. associationism   B. behaviorism
    C. Gestalt psychology   D. functionalism

14. Which one of the following is an example of "projection"?

    A. Calling other people hostile although the hostility is within oneself
    B. Playing sick in order to avoid responsibility
    C. Kicking the desk when one really wants to kick the teacher
    D. Giving other than the true reason for one's behavior

15. The basketball player who was dropped from the squad says, "Now I'll have time to study." If he really wanted to make the team, he is

    A. regressing   B. repressing
    C. projecting   D. rationalizing

16. Which one of the following reactions is generally instigated by frustration?

    A. Tolerance
    B. Aggression
    C. Identification
    D. Avoidance

17. A patient asserts, "I can't stand the agony I suffer when I go against my mother's wishes." The therapist replies, "You really like to punish that momma inside of you for your dependency, don't you?" This response can be viewed as an example of

    A. reassurance
    B. interpretation
    C. support
    D. reflection of feeling

18. A shy young first-grade boy becomes extremely attached to his teacher. He brings her presents, asks her to help him with his clothing a great deal, and wants to sit near her all the time. He is MOST likely manifesting the mental mechanism of

    A. introjection
    B. sublimation
    C. reaction-formation
    D. transference

19. When Billy was told he could not have a cookie, he lay down on the floor and pounded it with his fists. This could be an example of

    A. repression
    B. inhibition
    C. overcompensation
    D. regression

20. Habit formations in children such biting nails, picking at sores, masturbating, etc. are generally the result of

    A. poor parental supervision and training
    B. local irritations
    C. impaired general health
    D. emotional tensions

21. The attention span of a young child

    A. is not related to his mental ability
    B. can be increased if he has a high I.Q.
    C. cannot be changed before the child learns to read
    D. can be increased if the child is interested in what he is doing

22. Most young children need

    A. few media of expression
    B. to engage in independent planning
    C. many concrete experiences
    D. generalized explanations

23. The person with whom it is MOST important for a five-year-old child to have a good adjustment is

    A. father
    B. mother
    C. teacher
    D. sibling

24. At five, the normal, average child is able to play BEST

    A. alone
    B. in a large group
    C. with one other child somewhat older than himself
    D. in a small group of five or six children

25. Good education for five-year-old children stresses the importance of

    A. learning to sit still and wait for a turn
    B. opportunities to develop skill in crafts
    C. opportunities to explore and experiment
    D. learning to walk with a partner in line

26. Motor activities figure MOST importantly in a young child's intellectual enterprises because, through them, he

    A. learns how to meet new situations successfully
    B. acquires concepts of size, shape, balance, proportion
    C. learns how to live happily with other children
    D. gains confidence in himself as a person

27. Children can BEST be helped to make good choices through

    A. play with peers
    B. many experiences in making choices
    C. absorbing the teacher's sense of values
    D. imitating other children older than they

28. The timid, shy child who hesitates to join in activities and use of materials

    A. should be left alone
    B. should be praised for the work he does by himself
    C. should be drawn into the group and encouraged to participate as often as possible
    D. should have his mother come to his class to visit so that he will have a feeling of security

29. To understand the emotional life of the adolescent, it is MOST important to

    A. appraise the adolescent's emotions in the light of our own experience
    B. take into account the many forces, apparent as well as hidden, that operate in his life
    C. overlook impulsive behavior without apparent motive
    D. draw up a scholastic profile

30. The youngster who says, "I got an A in mathematics, but the teacher gave me a D in reading," is manifesting behavior which may be termed

    A. identification   B. projection
    C. regression   D. repression

31. Of the following comments which might be made by a teacher to a boy who has just misbehaved, the one likely to be MOST effective in correcting the behavior is:

    A. You are a bad boy who likes to misbehave.
    B. You are a silly boy and don't know how to behave.
    C. You are a poor, foolish boy who will get in trouble.
    D. You are a good boy but you made a mistake.

32. The personality development of young children is hampered MOST by

    A. the lack of good schools manned by adequately educated teachers
    B. dissension in the family
    C. the lack of love and affection
    D. failure in school

33. It has been found that the gap between ability and achievement is generally SMALLEST in the

    A. gifted pupil
    B. dull pupil
    C. average pupil
    D. pupil of high socio-economic background

34. Extreme deviations in motor, adaptive, or language expression or personal-social behavior are

    A. a definite indication that a child is subnormal
    B. cause for alarm on the part of parent and teacher
    C. an indication of a temporary maladjustment
    D. reasons for seeking the advice of a specialist

35. Children's groups about the age of two typically show

    A. much cooperation
    B. sex segregation
    C. parallel activity
    D. all of these

36. Play and reading interests of boys and girls will be found to be MOST different at the age of

    A. three years
    B. six years
    C. ten years
    D. twelve years

37. As children in groups with very limited environments, such as canal-boat dwellers, "hollow-folk," etc., grow older, their I.Q. is found to

    A. increase
    B. increase greatly
    C. stay the same
    D. decrease

38. Transfer from one subject to another or to life situations will be increased if

    A. techniques and applications are emphasized
    B. the first subject is very difficult
    C. a good deal of drill is given in the first subject
    D. the situations seem quite different

39. A contemporary book by Sheldon and Eleanor Glueck reports their findings of a careful research study of juvenile delinquents. They state that

    A. most of their delinquents showed anti-social behavior beginning with their sixth year
    B. most of their delinquents did not show anti-social behavior until after their eleventh year
    C. the delinquents showed more physical defects than non-delinquents
    D. prediction tables can help to detect potential delinquents

40. Finger sucking in early childhood has long been a subject of discussion among psychiatrists. The one of the following statements which is GENERALLY accepted as true is that
    A. finger sucking denotes pending neuroses and the parents need psychiatric consultation
    B. finger sucking is a normal activity of early childhood and should not be interfered with
    C. finger sucking alters the child's facial contours and should be heavily discouraged
    D. finger sucking by a child over nine months old is due to emotional upset and needs treatment

KEY (CORRECT ANSWERS)

1. B	11. D	21. D	31. D
2. A	12. B	22. C	32. C
3. A	13. C	23. B	33. B
4. B	14. A	24. D	34. D
5. A	15. D	25. C	35. C
6. D	16. B	26. B	36. D
7. D	17. B	27. B	37. D
8. B	18. D	28. C	38. A
9. C	19. D	29. B	39. D
10. B	20. D	30. B	40. B

42

EXAMINATION SECTION
TEST 1

DIRECTIONS: Each question or incomplete statement is followed by several suggested answers or completions. Select the one that BEST answers the question or completes the statement. *PRINT THE LETTER OF THE CORRECT ANSWER IN THE SPACE AT THE RIGHT.*

1. Of the following, the area of greatest similarity among children is in their

    A. inherited traits
    B. rates of development
    C. sequences of development
    D. patterns of growth dimensions
    E. perceptual and conceptual development

2. Of the following, which is the MOST significant factor in determining the choice of friends among children between the ages of six and ten?

    A. Mutual interests
    B. Similar personality traits
    C. Conveniently close location
    D. Social and economic standing of parents
    E. Physical maturity

3. Joe Flirp is a great health education teacher, to a large extent, because the boys model themselves after him. The foregoing illustrates the psychological mechanism of

    A. sublimation   B. displacement
    C. regression   D. identification
    E. projection

4. "You're much too authoritarian," said the principal to the teacher. "And I won't stand for that in my school." The principal is demonstrating the psychological mechanism of

    A. sublimation   B. conversion
    C. projection   D. identification
    E. displaced aggression

5. Margaret Snorble, unhappy because of her lack of friendship, devoted all her energy to studying. She became the number one student in her grade. Margaret is demonstrating the psychological mechanism of

    A. sublimation   B. conversion
    C. introjection   D. fantasy
    E. rationalization

6. Joanie asked for apple pie and was told that there was none left. "Oh well," said she, "give me peach pie. I like it better anyway." Joanie is demonstrating the psychological mechanism of

    A. regression   B. displacement
    C. rationalization   D. sublimation
    E. recidivism

7. The principal had just left after telling Miss Jones she had to improve the quality of her lesson plans. Tears came to her eyes; she stamped her foot several times, pounded on the desk and then broke into uncontrolled sobbing. Miss Jones' behavior is an example of the psychological mechanism of

   A. introjection
   B. projection
   C. sublimation
   D. regression
   E. displaced hostility

8. Of the following statements concerning praise and punishment, which is LEAST in accord with modern psychological principles?

   A. When a child is bad, spank him.
   B. When a child is bad, say, "If you're not good, I won't love you any more."
   C. When a child is good, give him something to show your approval.
   D. When a child is good, say, "That's O.K. Let's try to do better next time."
   E. When a child is good, do not over-reinforce him.

9. Defining personality as the end-product of our habit systems expresses a concept most characteristic of a psychological orientation termed

   A. behavioristic
   B. psychoanalytic
   C. Gestalt
   D. personalistic
   E. structuralistic

10. Studies on intelligence and creativity have yielded findings which indicate that

    A. the two characteristics are completely independent
    B. they are independent for subjects of high average ability and above
    C. they are negatively correlated
    D. for all practical purposes, measuring one trait is essentially the same as measuring the other
    E. the two characteristics vary in pattern, depending on the particular individual being tested

11. A five-year-old is walking with his father and notes that there is a full moon. He says, "Daddy, the moon is following us." What type of thinking is exemplified by the child's comment?

    A. Syncretism
    B. Centralism
    C. Autism
    D. Primatism
    E. Egocentrism

12. The process whereby an individual develops great sympathy towards another in order to conceal from himself certain malicious feelings toward this person, is known as

    A. rationalization
    B. intropunitiveness
    C. extrapunitiveness
    D. reaction formation
    E. introjection

13. Paranoia is best understood in terms of the mechanism of

    A. projection
    B. regression
    C. hostility
    D. reaction formation
    E. sublimation

14. The MOST practicable procedure yet found to identify persons who are not giving honest answers in a personality inventory is to

    A. include a set of items which sound good but which few honest persons would answer in the "good" direction
    B. repeat the inventory at a later date
    C. check the consistency of the response to different items
    D. tell the individual to try to make himself appear normal, then neurotic
    E. repeat certain questions in slightly different form throughout the test

14.____

15. Johnny, a twelve-year-old handicapped child, suddenly begins to suck his thumb and wet his bed soon after his newborn brother is brought home from the hospital. This psychological mechanism is known as

    A. introjection
    B. sublimation
    C. repression
    D. regression
    E. compensation

15.____

16. Six- and seven-year-old children are interested primarily in stories about

    A. family and school activities
    B. fairies and elves
    C. adventures on land and sea
    D. science and nature
    E. cowboys and Indians

16.____

17. The use of rewards is MOST productive in learning to the extent that they

    A. are concrete
    B. are used economically
    C. are delayed
    D. correspond to the work that has been done
    E. fulfill a need of the learner

17.____

18. In order to increase the chances that learned responses will be applied to new problem situations, the teacher should attempt, whenever possible, to

    A. provide clear objectives
    B. use concrete materials
    C. generalize patterns of response
    D. integrate subject matter areas
    E. use examples from everyday life

18.____

19. The pupil's readiness for any learning situation is the sum of all his characteristics which make him more likely to respond one way than another. Of these characteristics, the MOST important one generally is his

    A. interests
    B. physical health
    C. previous experience
    D. maturity
    E. perceptivity

19.____

20. It is generally assumed by clinical psychologists that the MOST serious behavior problems are manifested by children who

20.____

A.	are most retarded	B.	are most withdrawn
C.	are most aggressive	D.	cannot read
E.	are overly dependent		

21. Finger painting is enjoyed by many children. As a mechanism of adjustment, interest in finger painting may be looked upon as a form of

    A. projection
    B. conversion
    C. self-expression
    D. sublimation
    E. displacement

22. Personal problems in adjustment are MOST likely to arise in adolescent groups of

    A. early maturing girls and boys
    B. late maturing girls and boys
    C. early maturing girls and late maturing boys
    D. late maturing girls and early maturing boys
    E. all early and late maturing girls and boys

23. In establishing identity and sex role, the adolescent is MOST likely to be influenced by

    A. parents
    B. siblings
    C. peers
    D. ministers
    E. movie and baseball stars

24. Which one of the following judgments about parent-teenager relationships is FALSE?

    A. A parent's approval of work well done and overt pride in his child's accomplishment mean a great deal to the teenager, even though the latter may make light of it.
    B. To enhance ultimately the young person's self-respect, it is a good idea to criticize and question him as much as possible.
    C. Giving a teenager abundant opportunity to relate with a group has a positive effect on his school achievement.
    D. A parent's recognition and appreciation of good school progress, without exerting heavy pressure, serves to aid in maintaining this good record of accomplishment.
    E. A parent's realization that a major aspect of adolescent social development is the shift in interest and involvement from the family to the outside, with a concomitant desire and need for independence.

25. In learning theory terms, the psychoanalytic mechanism of displacement may be seen as an illustration of

    A. reinforcement
    B. discrimination
    C. extinction
    D. generalization
    E. assimilation

26. When an illness is described as psychosomatic, it means that the symptoms

    A. are psychological, but physiological factors contribute
    B. are physiological, but psychological factors contribute
    C. and all contributing factors are psychological
    D. and all contributing factors are physiological
    E. are both physiological and psychological

27. Most pronounced cases of bullying and aggressiveness are the result of efforts on the child's part to

A. impress adults with his strength
B. gain the attention of those around him
C. reach a level of achievement that is beyond him
D. compensate for deep feelings of inadequacy
E. create a "real-self" which corresponds to an "ideal-self"

28. Suzanne has received more votes than any other girl for student senate member. If she is typical of most of the girls who win this kind of recognition, she probably differs MOST from the average girl in the school in

    A. being emotionally more mature and balanced
    B. showing less competitive and aggressive tendencies
    C. making innovations without permission
    D. exhibiting more concern for herself and less awareness of the needs and problems of others
    E. being somewhat superior in aptitude and achievement

28.____

29. "I know what my parents expect of me; I know what teachers demand. I know what the other fellows in my crowd want me to do. I have a dim idea of what my girl wants from me. But I don't know what I want for myself." This statement illustrates the central adolescent problem of

    A. configuration
    B. peer group conformity
    C. acculturation
    D. introspection and inversion
    E. identity

29.____

30. The imaginative transposing of oneself into the thinking, feeling, and acting of another, and so structuring the world as he does, is an accurate definition of

    A. empathy   B. rapport
    C. conditioning   D. exclusion
    E. projection

30.____

31. A common change in the personality defenses of the adolescent child is the development of

    A. greater intellectualism and isolation of affect
    B. a tendency toward avoidance and denial
    C. suspicion and withdrawal
    D. repression and depression
    E. greater empathy and awareness of others

31.____

32. Tom has applied for several college scholarships, but has not obtained any. He says that none of the colleges really examine the candidates carefully or fairly. Which defense mechanism is he manifesting? That of

    A. rationalization   B. projection
    C. sublimation   D. repression
    E. introspection

32.____

33. When a person says, "I am so fond of you," when you know he actually dislikes you, there is reason to suspect that he is using the defense mechanism of

33.____

A. introjection
C. rationalization
E. reaction formation
B. projection
D. compensation

34. Of the following self-concepts, the MOST desirable one for a child to develop from the standpoint of mental health is

   A. whatever I do is good
   B. if I fail at something, it isn't important
   C. I know I have limitations; no one is perfect
   D. I must always be alert to my weaknesses
   E. I am capable of reaching my goals

35. Studies of children's fantasies show that, in the average elementary school child, fantasies

   A. play no significant part in his life
   B. will still be active but are becoming tempered with reality
   C. are an indication of an unsettled inner life
   D. are an indication that the child is unable to face his problems
   E. encourage the child to retreat from the demands of the world of reality

36. In collecting data for identifying pupil problems, information which compares a child to his peer group is called

   A. ideographic
   C. psychodiagnostic
   E. sociometric
   B. psychogenic
   D. normative

37. Of the following, what is the effect of a child's self-concept upon his behavior?

   A. It shifts and/or distorts the perceptions that act as stimuli to behavior.
   B. It functions principally in matters where conformity to or violation of the social code is involved.
   C. Its influence is best described by the Freudian concept of superego.
   D. It enables him to put his best foot forward.
   E. It helps the child to learn who he really is.

38. Compared to a group of unselected children of the same age, sex and race, gifted children, on the average,

   A. have a higher incidence of visual defects
   B. reach puberty later
   C. are taller, heavier and stronger
   D. show more personality problems
   E. are better "mixers"

39. Roger, who has a morbid fear of attending school and has been absent all year, is described as suffering from a(n)

   A. psychosis
   C. inversion
   E. psychopathy
   B. phobia
   D. regression

40. The term AMBIVALENT is used to describe a child who 40.____

    A. is given to creating dissension among others
    B. makes a statement and later amplifies it with conscious intent
    C. seems to be daydreaming while actually alert
    D. is aggressive at times and friendly at other times
    E. fearful in manner but overpowering in action

41. Transference is an important aspect of 41.____

    A. test construction
    B. grade placement
    C. anecdotal record keeping
    D. superior intelligence
    E. therapy

42. The term commonly used in statistics to refer to the average of a group of scores is the 42.____

    A. range   B. mode
    C. central tendency   D. median
    E. mean

43. A wound or injury to the emotions is called 43.____

    A. an illusion   B. a trauma
    C. hysteria   D. a delusion
    E. a syndrome

44. A child is psychotic who has a(n) 44.____

    A. urge toward some inappropriate sexual behavior
    B. nervous disorder of a functional type
    C. prolonged form of mental derangement
    D. inhibition in his social behavior
    E. physiogenic disorder

45. Individual differences in persons begin to be noticeable 45.____

    A. from birth onward
    B. after the child enters school
    C. when the child begins to communicate
    D. after visual-motor coordination has been achieved
    E. when the child begins to participate in competitive sports

46. In which one of the following statements is the mechanism of identification operating? 46.____

    A. "I'm not a good ballplayer, but I get good grades in arithmetic."
    B. "My teacher is always picking on me."
    C. "John was mad at me, but I'm bigger, so he pushed Sally, she's smaller."
    D. "I like blue dresses; my teacher wears blue a lot."
    E. "Of course I lost the tennis match; I was using a defective racket!"

47. In developing good character traits in young children, the BEST of the following techniques is probably 47.____

A. short dramatic discussions on good behavior
B. TV programs which have good behavior as "the moral"
C. administration of a personality test and follow-up discussion of the results
D. the desired type of behavior on the part of the adults with whom the children come into contact regularly
E. the emulation of outstanding personalities in the news, including athletes and actors

48. The term which MOST clearly expresses the psychological basis of modern educational practice is

A. atomistic
B. structuralistic
C. analytic
D. behavioristic
E. organismic

49. Of the following possible first steps for helping an awkward child overcome his fear of playground activities, the one which is usually BEST is to

A. give him some easy task connected with the game, "keeping score," for example
B. send him to another classroom during the game period
C. insist that he get into the game and play immediately
D. allow him to work or do something else, alone
E. encourage him to observe the game for a while with the hope that he will soon be motivated to play

50. Of the following, the MOST important consideration in distinguishing anxiety from fear is the

A. intensity of the emotion
B. extent of relation to subjective as distinguished from objective conditions
C. strength of the personality organization of the one who is affected
D. actuality of danger
E. direction of the emotion

KEY (CORRECT ANSWERS)

1. C	11. E	21. D	31. A	41. E
2. C	12. D	22. C	32. A	42. E
3. D	13. A	23. C	33. E	43. B
4. C	14. A	24. B	34. E	44. C
5. A	15. D	25. D	35. B	45. A
6. C	16. A	26. B	36. D	46. D
7. D	17. E	27. D	37. A	47. D
8. B	18. C	28. C	38. C	48. E
9. A	19. D	29. E	39. B	49. A
10. B	20. B	30. A	40. D	50. B

TEST 2

DIRECTIONS: Each question or incomplete statement is followed by several suggested answers or completions. Select the one that BEST answers the question or completes the statement. *PRINT THE LETTER OF THE CORRECT ANSWER IN THE SPACE AT THE RIGHT.*

1. Research on sex differences in reading achievement indicates that   1.____

   A. more boys than girls suffer reading disabilities
   B. more girls than boys suffer reading disabilities
   C. there are no appreciable sex differences in reading achievement
   D. more boys than girls suffer reading disabilities in the elementary grades, but more girls than boys suffer reading disabilities in the secondary grades
   E. all such studies are statistically unreliable

2. Studies have shown that the ratio of reading disability among boys as compared to girls is   2.____

   A. 4 to 1   B. 3 to 1
   C. 2 to 1   D. equal
   E. slightly greater

3. The pecularities of language behavior in the schizophrenic arise from his extreme need of a feeling of   3.____

   A. personal security   B. self-denial
   C. disarticulation   D. isolation
   E. grandeur

4. Of the following, the LEAST effective way of dealing with children's fears is   4.____

   A. explaining and reassuring
   B. helping the child to face the feared situation
   C. simply ignoring the child's fear
   D. setting examples of fearlessness
   E. looking to the causes of the fear

5. The age at which individuals cease to grow in intellectual ability is   5.____

   A. 13 years   B. 16 years
   C. 21 years   D. 29 years
   E. probably none of these

6. Personality is the result of   6.____

   A. inheritance only
   B. environment only
   C. both inheritance and environment
   D. neither inheritance nor environment
   E. inheritance to a greater extent than environment

7. Children's groups about the age of two typically show

   A. much cooperation B. sex segregation
   C. parallel activity D. all of these
   E. none of these

8. Play and reading interests of boys and girls will be found to be MOST different at the age of

   A. three years B. six years
   C. ten years D. twelve years
   E. eighteen years

9. As children in groups with very limited environments, such as canal-boat dwellers, "hollow-folk," etc., grow older, their I.Q. is found to

   A. increase
   B. increase greatly
   C. stay the same
   D. decrease
   E. vary widely and irregularly

10. A child reared in isolation will NOT naturally

    A. eat
    B. sleep
    C. talk
    D. take shelter
    E. investigate his surroundings

11. Although young children are egocentric, it has been found that social development

    A. is common among two-year-olds
    B. is well under way at the age of four
    C. is well under way at the age of five
    D. is not noticeable until the sixth-year level
    E. varies so greatly among children that it cannot be approximated at any one age

12. The rate and pattern of early motor development of children depend *mainly* upon

    A. experience B. acculturation
    C. maturation D. training
    E. personal aptitude

13. For optimum individual and social growth, children should be encouraged to

    A. initiate their own activities
    B. accept the choices and decisions of their peers
    C. learn to play alone
    D. respect the leaders in the class
    E. participate in clubs and groups led by children of their own age

14. Most young adolescents

    A. struggle to establish themselves as important members of the family but question family controls
    B. struggle to establish themselves as important members of the family and accept family controls without question
    C. are content with secondary roles in the family provided the family relinquishes all controls over them
    D. prefer to be told what to do by parents in order to be relieved of all responsibility for making decisions
    E. accept family controls when the rules are set by the father, but question and often disobey controls set by the mother

15. Because boys and girls of junior high school age become increasingly interested in the opposite sex, the teacher should

    A. seat them apart so that they can concentrate on their work
    B. encourage "dating"
    C. group the students with members of their own sex for all committee work
    D. forbid the use of all cosmetics in class
    E. teach the social amenities

16. On the whole, if junior high school children are treated as responsible young people,

    A. they will do what is expected of them
    B. they will react by giggling
    C. the teacher will lose control of the class
    D. their parents will object because they are not yet ready for responsibility
    E. they will assume that they are not amenable to ordinary school regulations

17. The adolescent is MOST likely to seek the greatest emotional support and understanding from

    A. idealized adults   B. isolated activity
    C. religious authorities   D. heterosexual interactions
    E. the peer culture

18. Emotional reactions are so important in behavior disorders because they are

    A. very intense
    B. not readily changed from infancy to adulthood
    C. varying in form from person to person
    D. so easily learned
    E. difficult to communicate and share socially

19. At the adolescent level, "adjustment" usually depends MOST strongly on having

    A. respect from parents
    B. adequate sex education
    C. average school achievement or better
    D. warm approval from teachers
    E. acceptance from peers

20. The fantasies of a child are MOST often used by a psychologist as a clue to his
    A. level of maturity
    B. inner needs
    C. social adjustment
    D. intelligence
    E. emotional stability

21.
    I. The social and emotional adjustment of the child of six to eight depends in a major way on the security of the home.
    II. Children tend to form stereotypes and to focus on the unusual.
    The CORRECT answer is:
    A. Both I and II are correct
    B. Both I and II are incorrect
    C. I is correct; II is incorrect
    D. I is incorrect; II is correct
    E. One cannot draw a conclusion

22. The psychological climate of the home which influences adjustment of the child is MOST closely related to the
    A. number of children in the home
    B. educational level of the parents
    C. occupational level of the father
    D. attitudes of the parents
    E. socio-economic status of the family

23. Of the following characteristics, the one MOST generally found among children just entering the junior high schools is
    A. a tendency of boys and girls to seek each other's company
    B. the acceptance of parent and teacher opinion with little question
    C. the popularity of guessing games, puzzles, and games of choice
    D. a preference for highly organized competitive team play
    E. a conscientious and ardent effort to achieve academic success

24. Studies of child growth indicate that
    A. the onset of puberty adversely effects the child's motor coordination
    B. mentally retarded children are usually above norms in physical growth
    C. each child has his own growth pattern
    D. mental growth and physical growth are highly correlated
    E. physical growth and emotional stability are highly correlated

25. Which of the following statements is LEAST likely to be TRUE of first grade children as compared with fifth graders?
    A. There is much concern for group welfare and group approval.
    B. There is little concern for order and neatness.
    C. Some regular routines give security to children of this age.
    D. There is little intermingling of boys and girls in their play activities.
    E. There is a dislike for oral reading.

26. Most differences in play activities and interests between boys and girls in the elementary school years can probably be attributed to   26.____

    A. inherent biological differences
    B. inherent emotional differences
    C. instinctual influences
    D. cultural influences
    E. inherent intellectual differences

27. As part of the socialization process, the phenomenon of ambivalence is at its highest intensity during the   27.____

    A. toddler years
    B. preschool years
    C. early school years
    D. intermediate school years
    E. high school years

28. In early childhood, the individual tends to pattern himself on or to identify himself MOST generally with   28.____

    A. glamorous or romantic figures
    B. age contemporaries
    C. characters in movies or on TV
    D. parents or parent substitutes
    E. teachers

29. With respect to physical growth, superior children as compared with children of average intelligence are   29.____

    A. markedly inferior   B. slightly inferior
    C. slightly superior   D. about average
    E. markedly superior

30. Wishes of children of elementary school age deal mainly with   30.____

    A. improvement of their own inner strength, character or intelligence
    B. exploitation of family relationships
    C. possessions, pleasant experiences, privileges, opportunities for enjoyment
    D. improvement of their personal appearance
    E. improvement of their physical strength and prowess

31. With reference to emotional stability, intellectually gifted children as a group compared to average children are   31.____

    A. generally inferior   B. unpredictably related
    C. generally superior   D. predictably related
    E. the same

32. In comparing the rate of biological growth for boys and girls between the ages of 5-7 and 7-10, the latter period shows   32.____

    A. a slightly more accelerated rate than the former
    B. a slightly less accelerated rate than the former
    C. a rate equal to the former period

D. a markedly more accelerated rate than the former
E. a markedly less accelerated rate than the former

33. Of the following, the MOST important determinant of leadership in pre-adolescent children is the child's
    A. self-confidence
    B. sex
    C. physical attractiveness
    D. socio-economic status
    E. mental abilities

34. Marked improvement in a child's ability to draw a man over a period of time is MOST likely to be related to
    A. better social adjustment
    B. maturational effect
    C. the overcoming of a reading disability
    D. recovery from an illness
    E. better muscular coordination

35. As a means of changing the current behavior pattern of an adolescent, which of the following forces will generally prove to be MOST potent? Disapproval of the behavior pattern by
    A. the adolescent's parents
    B. an adult he admires
    C. a group of his peers
    D. his classroom teacher
    E. a close sibling

36. Of the following, the characteristic that is MOST important in determining an individual's status in a group of pre-adolescent girls is her
    A. school achievement
    B. socio-economic status
    C. ability to make friends
    D. intelligence
    E. physical appearance

37. The main advantage of the cross-sectional study over the longitudinal study in child development research is that the former
    A. permits an analysis of the growth of each child
    B. allows for an examination of individual and child growth increments
    C. allows for a detailed analysis of the interrelations among growth processes
    D. involves fewer sampling difficulties
    E. yields more accurate results by studying a larger sample

38. The greatest "social distance" in boy-girl relationships has been found to be during the ages
    A. 13 to 17 years
    B. 9 to 13 years
    C. 2 to 5 years
    D. 5 to 9 years
    E. 17 to 19 years

39. Of the following, the MOST frequent reason why two 11-year old boys stop "being friends" is

    A. lack of agreement concerning activities to be undertaken
    B. lack of recent contact
    C. parental disapproval
    D. a clash of personalities
    E. changing interests

40. A recent comprehensive survey of child-rearing patterns in America found mothers of the working class when compared in their toilet-training practices with mothers of the upper-middle class to be

    A. more permissive
    B. more accepting
    C. more severe
    D. more indifferent
    E. more uninformed

41. The leisure time activities of the typical pre-adolescent boys' group is mainly given over to

    A. a succession of activities suited to a changing number of players
    B. just "hanging around with the boys"
    C. games governed by a highly organized series of rules
    D. aimless circulation over a relatively large area looking for something to do
    E. a succession of activities suited to a limited number of players and games governed by few, if any, rules

42. Of the following, the MOST important symptom indicative of the social and emotional maladjustment of problem pupils is

    A. whispering and fooling while work is going on
    B. association with a gang
    C. destroying your neighbor's work
    D. inability to assume responsibility
    E. shyness and daydreaming

43. Of the following types of behavior, psychiatrists consider the MOST serious to be

    A. profanity
    B. smoking
    C. unsociability
    D. whispering in class
    E. dependence

44. The MOST impelling reason for young adolescents' use of slang is

    A. ignorance
    B. hearing it at home
    C. the desire to attain peer status through its use
    D. the attraction of its colorful expressions
    E. rebellion against the accepted media of speech

45. Sibling rivalry is the term used to describe the competitive feeling between two or more individuals who

    A. are in the same school grade
    B. are children of the same parents
    C. have similar goals of achievement
    D. are in the same chronological age group
    E. are identical twins

45.___

KEY (CORRECT ANSWERS)

1. A	11. B	21. A	31. C	41. A
2. B	12. B	22. D	32. B	42. B
3. A	13. B	23. C	33. A	43. C
4. C	14. A	24. C	34. A	44. C
5. E	15. E	25. A	35. C	45. B
6. C	16. A	26. D	36. C	
7. C	17. E	27. B	37. D	
8. D	18. E	28. D	38. B	
9. D	19. E	29. C	39. B	
10. C	20. B	30. C	40. C	

EXAMINATION SECTION
TEST 1

DIRECTIONS: Each question or incomplete statement is followed by several suggested answers or completions. Select the one that BEST answers the question or completes the statement. *PRINT THE LETTER OF THE CORRECT ANSWER IN THE SPACE AT THE RIGHT.*

1. Which one of the following statements is TRUE with respect to the development of language ability?

    A. Boys tend to talk a little earlier than girls.
    B. Twins tend to talk earlier than single children.
    C. The amount of stimulation in the home environment is a relatively unimportant factor in the development of language.
    D. Children who talk earliest generally prove to be most intelligent when tested at a later age.

2. Which of the following statements is LEAST likely to be TRUE of first-grade children as compared with fifth graders?

    A. There is much concern for group welfare and group approval.
    B. There is little concern for order and neatness.
    C. Some regular routines give security to children of this age.
    D. There is little intermingling of boys and girls in their play activities.

3. Reasoning begins to develop in children during the period of the _____ years.

    A. pre-school   B. primary school
    C. intermediate school   D. high school

4. Growth

    A. is saltatory
    B. proceeds most rapidly during the adolescent years
    C. follows an orderly genetic sequence in the emergence of behavior patterns
    D. depends entirely on maturation

5. When the individual perceives relationships, observes which things belong together, and which things do not, or observes the relation between means and ends, he is said to

    A. introspect   B. remember
    C. learn by "insight"   D. possess eidetic imagery

6. Investigators have found a small but consistent superiority of females over males in _____ ability.

    A. artistic   B. linguistic
    C. arithmetical   D. reasoning

7. Mental development and physical development are _____ correlated.

    A. highly   B. perfectly
    C. only very slightly   D. not in the least

8. Which of the following statements is MOST in agreement with modern theories of child development? Growth is a(n)

   A. continuous process, uniform in rate
   B. continuous process, but it is not uniform in rate
   C. predictable process, but so highly individual that group generalizations should not be attempted
   D. unpredictable process in which patterns are difficult to establish

9. Generally, which of the following influences exerts the GREATEST impact on the development of the self-concept in fifteen-year-old individuals?

   A. Acceptance by their friends and classmates
   B. Acceptance by their teachers
   C. Ideals and aspirations
   D. Knowledge of their abilities from school experiences

10. In comparing boys and girls as to the period of peak body growth, called the "prepuberal growth spurt," it can be said that, on the average,

    A. girls precede boys by about eighteen months
    B. the phenomenon occurs in both sexes at about the same time
    C. boys precede girls by about one year
    D. girls precede boys by about six months

11. As a child grows older, outwardly visible signs of emotion become

    A. more intense
    B. more common
    C. less frequent
    D. less important

12. Fairy tales are MOST popular with children whose age is

    A. 3 years
    B. 5 years
    C. 7 years
    D. 9 years

13. Of the following, the MOST suitable active game for seven-year-old children is

    A. London Bridge
    B. Looby-Loo
    C. dodge ball
    D. Cobbler, Mend My Shoe

14. All of the following are characteristic of the typical four-year-old EXCEPT

    A. his attention span is short
    B. his coordination is not well-developed
    C. he is not likely to be interested in people
    D. he is not likely to share things with other children

15. Of the following physical characteristics of the pre-kindergarten child, the one which is INCORRECT is that he

    A. begins to develop small muscle control
    B. is susceptible to communicable diseases
    C. is usually near-sighted
    D. needs frequent rest

16. Of the following, the GREATEST factor in the motor development of a five-year-old child is

    A. steady practice
    B. mental ability
    C. maturation
    D. home environment

17. Of the following, the statement which BEST describes the child of kindergarten age is that he

    A. is adept at projecting himself into other places and times
    B. is incapable of any flights of imagination
    C. seldom questions anything in his physical environment
    D. is bound to the here and now by his stage of organic development, as well as by his limited experience

18. Of the following, the PRIME reason why five-year-olds are often willing to share their things is that they

    A. seek adult approval
    B. have no interest in possessions
    C. have no use for them
    D. prefer companions to possessions

19. Research tends to show that all of the following are TRUE of development of language in children of pre-school and elementary school age EXCEPT that

    A. girls tend to be poorer than boys in clarity of enunciation and freedom from speech defects
    B. the number of basic words known increases by several thousands per year
    C. the length of responses tends to increase with the age of the child
    D. the average length of sentences spoken by girls is greater than it is for boys of the same age

20. Of the following, the natural sequence of language growth is

    A. listening, reading, speaking, writing
    B. reading, listening, speaking, writing
    C. listening, speaking, reading, writing
    D. listening, speaking, writing, reading

21. Of the following parts of speech, the one which predominates in the vocabulary of a child beginning to speak is

    A. adjectives
    B. nouns
    C. verbs
    D. pronouns

22. All of the following are known for writings in the area of child growth and development EXCEPT

    A. Frances Ilg
    B. Anna B. Comstock
    C. Arnold Gesell
    D. Maria Montessori

23. All of the following are characteristic of the average seven-year-old EXCEPT that he

    A. likes to bat and pitch a ball
    B. fits easily into organized group play

C. enjoys alternate periods of activity and inactivity
D. shows more interest in some activities and tries fewer new ventures than the four-year-old

24. All of the following statements regarding language arts in early childhood education are true EXCEPT

   A. if a number of children wander away while the teacher is reading a story, it may be that they have had too many sedentary activities that day
   B. storytelling - as opposed to story reading - should be undertaken only when the teacher feels she is unable to read the story with sufficient dramatic expression to maintain the children's interest
   C. listening to rhythmic poetry affords much enjoyment to young children
   D. the line between fantasy and reality is generally not sharply defined in the mind of the four-year-old child

25. All of the following statements concerning social relationships in the early school years are usually true EXCEPT

   A. groups are small and shift rapidly
   B. friends are selected because of propinquity and the accident of sharing objects
   C. children play and work with others to satisfy personal rather than social desires
   D. friends are selected on the basis of belonging to the same sex

26. In general, the language development of girls is

   A. more rapid than that of boys
   B. less rapid than that of boys
   C. equal to that of boys
   D. more rapid than that of boys in oral communication, but slower in written communication

27. Defense mechanisms are used

   A. *most frequently* by average children
   B. *less frequently* by slow learners than by average children
   C. *more frequently* by slow learners than by average children
   D. *by all children* regardless of level of ability

28. Research in child development shows that all children have

   A. a single, fixed design of growth
   B. individual potentialities for various patterns of growth
   C. equal abilities for growth in all areas
   D. no consistent growth patterns

29. The period designated as "early childhood"

   A. is a period when memory is high
   B. is a time of very rapid growth
   C. is relatively unimportant so far as learning is concerned
   D. is a time when there is little change in physical structure

30. Of the following, the one MOST characteristic of the normally developing adolescent is   30.____

    A. continuous need for parental support
    B. development of emotional maturity
    C. desire for constant domination by siblings
    D. freedom from peer group identification

31. The normal child on entering school knows the meaning of about   31.____

    A. 500 words   B. 1,000 words
    C. 2,000 words   D. 3,000 words

32. For a four-year-old child, the events of the present are   32.____

    A. less vivid than those of the past
    B. less vivid than those of the future
    C. more vivid than those of the past or future
    D. as vivid as those of the past or future

33. The EARLIEST aesthetic experiences of the young child are likely to occur in play with   33.____

    A. blocks and paints
    B. games and toys
    C. swings, see-saws, and sliding ponds
    D. kitchen and household utensils

34. Of the following characteristics of child development, the one MOST closely related to the 10-12 age group is   34.____

    A. difficulty with gross motor coordination
    B. eagerness for peer approval
    C. anxiety to please the teacher
    D. interest in the immediate environment

35. The one of the following which is a psychological principle which can BEST be described as a situation in which an individual experiences some ambivalence and indecisiveness in choosing one or more desired objects or goals is   35.____

    A. task-orientation   B. conflict
    C. apathy   D. projection

36. The treatment method which allows or encourages the client to express his charged feelings around a pressing emotional need is known as   36.____

    A. exploring   B. synthesizing
    C. catharsis   D. ventilating

37. The emotional release that results from recall of a previously forgotten painful experience is known as   37.____

    A. introjection   B. abreaction
    C. sublimation   D. free association

38. The action whereby an individual directs his aggression against an innocent bystander rather than expressing it against the source of his difficulties is called

    A. displacement
    B. projection
    C. introjection
    D. abreaction

39. An attempt to attribute emotionally caused behavior to reasonable factors MORE acceptable to the individual is known as

    A. projection
    B. rationalization
    C. introjection
    D. free association

40. The unconscious application of elements of the experiences in a former relationship to a new relationship is known as

    A. projection
    B. abreaction
    C. transference
    D. sublimation

41. In reference to learning, most children will tend to set goals for themselves which are

    A. similar to those of their peers
    B. different from those of their peers
    C. too difficult or complex
    D. too easy or too low

42. Children involved in initial learning tend to do significantly better on problems where the rule or principle is

    A. given or stated
    B. independently derived
    C. minimized
    D. neglected

43. Studies of sensory deprivation during infancy indicate that lack of stimulation during this period is most likely to result in

    A. low frustration tolerance
    B. poor psychomotor coordination
    C. lack of emotional responsiveness
    D. delayed intellectual development

44. When do coordination and convergence of the eyes begin to develop in the infant?

    A. Immediately after birth
    B. After one week
    C. After two weeks
    D. After three weeks

45. In the IOWA studies of children's reactions to frustration, which one of the following reactions was LEAST observed?

    A. Regression
    B. Aggression
    C. Resignation
    D. Accommodation

46. Dick, who is 14 years old, has been given a curfew of midnight. Arriving home at 2:30 A.M., he explains his decision to come in late was based on the fact that everyone his age stays out that late. He is using

    A. compensation
    B. denial
    C. displacement
    D. rationalization

47. By virtue of his earlier interaction with his mother, a child may display affectional responses to other adults.
    This is an example of

    A. secondary reinforcement
    B. stimulus generalization
    C. response diffusion
    D. learned mediation

48. Which one of the following BEST illustrates the distinction between "performance" and "competence" as drawn by contemporary psycholinguists?

    A. A child can vocalize before he can speak.
    B. A child's motor development depends upon language acquisition.
    C. A child is more limited in language production than in language comprehension.
    D. A child acquires language to meet his need to function as an effective person.

49. Bruner and Page, among others, contend that children can learn anything that adults can. Ausubel, in his writings,

    A. extends the contention
    B. modifies the contention
    C. rejects the contention
    D. supports the contention

50. An 8-year-old pupil is told by his teacher that he cannot join his group in play because he needs to practice writing. The boy starts crying, drops to the floor, sobs heavily and strikes the floor with hands and legs. The behavior exhibited by the boy is an example of

    A. repression
    B. identification
    C. aggression
    D. regression

KEY (CORRECT ANSWERS)

1.	D	11.	C	21.	B	31.	B	41.	A
2.	A	12.	C	22.	B	32.	C	42.	A
3.	A	13.	C	23.	B	33.	A	43.	D
4.	C	14.	C	24.	B	34.	B	44.	A
5.	C	15.	C	25.	A	35.	B	45.	D
6.	B	16.	C	26.	A	36.	D	46.	D
7.	C	17.	D	27.	D	37.	B	47.	B
8.	B	18.	A	28.	B	38.	A	48.	C
9.	A	19.	A	29.	B	39.	B	49.	C
10.	A	20.	C	30.	B	40.	C	50.	D

EXAMINATION SECTION
TEST 1

DIRECTIONS: Each question or incomplete statement is followed by several suggested answers or completions. Select the one that BEST answers the question or completes the statement. *PRINT THE LETTER OF THE CORRECT ANSWER IN THE SPACE AT THE RIGHT.*

1. The time of day MOST suitable for bathing a baby is

    A. just before feeding him
    B. just after feeding him
    C. early in the day
    D. at any time most convenient for the mother

2. Of the following, the BEST cure for diaper rash is to

    A. avoid the use of fabric softeners in laundering
    B. expose the rash to air and sunlight
    C. use waterproof pants over the diaper
    D. dry diapers slowly at a low temperature in laundering

3. Except for the consistency of food, the diet of a baby resembles that of an older child by the time he is _____ old.

    A. 6 weeks   B. 2 months   C. 3 months   D. 6 months

4. During the first three to five days of life, a normal baby loses

    A. two to three ounces of weight
    B. from several ounces to a pound of weight
    C. as much as two pounds of weight
    D. no weight

5. Toddlers at play

    A. generally amuse themselves
    B. need someone to play games with them
    C. need constant direction
    D. enjoy telling stories

6. During pregnancy, the first baby tooth starts to form during the _____ or _____ month.

    A. first; second   B. third; fourth
    C. sixth; seventh   D. eighth; ninth

7. The croup tent provides

    A. oxygen to relieve dyspnea
    B. warm moist air
    C. cool moist air
    D. cool dry air

8. Emetics used to reduce laryngeal spasms in croup are given PRIMARILY for the purpose of
   A. drying up bronchial secretions
   B. producing sleep
   C. inducing vomiting
   D. dilating the bronchi

9. An envelope-type wrap that covers a baby's hands and feet, as well as his body, is called a
   A. sacque
   B. Gertrude
   C. bunting
   D. crawler

10. The crust that sometimes forms on babies' scalps is called
    A. acne
    B. cradle cap
    C. eczema
    D. prickly heat

11. The MOST satisfactory filling for a crib mattress is
    A. cotton
    B. hair
    C. soft foam rubber
    D. cotton and innersprings

12. By far, the MOST common disrupter of the newborn's slumber is
    A. hunger pain
    B. his need for close, warm contact and rhythmic movement
    C. his need to exercise his lungs
    D. the *startle reflex*

13. Of the following, the MOST helpful when *burping* a baby at feeding is to
    A. thump him on the back
    B. avoid letting him suck on an empty bottle
    C. encourage relaxation by gentle patting or rubbing
    D. keep the bottle neck well-filled

14. The *soft spots* that can be felt in the newborn infant's skull are called the
    A. suture lines
    B. fontanels
    C. occipital sutures
    D. parietal cavities

15. A young baby's sleep position should be rotated in order to
    A. prevent misshaping of soft bones
    B. encourage him to roll from side to side
    C. make complete relaxation possible
    D. teach him to adjust

16. Of the following, the MOST advantageous sleep position for a baby is on his
    A. stomach
    B. back
    C. right side
    D. left side

17. In a newborn baby, the *Darwinian reflex*
    A. is set off by a touch on the child's lips
    B. gives the child an extra supply of oxygen
    C. is aroused by a sudden noise or loss of support
    D. makes the child's hands grasp anything touching his palm

18. The number of *milk* teeth which a baby usually has is

    A. 12 B. 16 C. 20 D. 24

19. In an infant, intense crying which nothing seems to help is PROBABLY a sign of

    A. colic
    B. indigestion
    C. too tightly binding garments
    D. possible injury from a pin

20. To habituate pupils in safety procedure,

    A. discuss the problem
    B. motivate them to want to practice safety
    C. insist on repetitive processes
    D. excuse occasional exceptions

21. Of the following, the STRONGEST influence on the personality of a child during his first three years is the

    A. playmates with whom he agrees
    B. economic status of the family
    C. social status of the family
    D. relationships with the members of his family

22. Of the following, the toy MOST suitable for a toddler is a(n)

    A. airplane
    B. pair of blunt scissors
    C. wheelbarrow
    D. small football

23. When a child becomes temporarily boisterous and irritable, the parents should

    A. divert his attention
    B. punish him
    C. cajol him
    D. try to ascertain the reason for the behavior

24. The BEST reason why school children should have a weekly allowance is that they may

    A. buy their own lunches
    B. learn how to use money
    C. learn to save money
    D. be popular with their friends

25. Among early indications of social consciousness of the infant, the FIRST is

    A. protest at being alone
    B. cooing at other infants
    C. the smile of recognition
    D. the demand for attention

26. A PRIMARY need of the infant is

    A. affection and security
    B. constant attention
    C. rigid regularity of schedule
    D. adequate discipline

27. Of the following, the LEAST satisfactory corrective measure when dealing with children is

    A. sending to bed   B. restriction
    C. isolation   D. deprivation

28. In a child's development, body control occurs FIRST in the muscles of the

    A. trunk   B. leg
    C. head   D. arm and hand

29. If a teenage girl is careless about putting her clothes away,

    A. put the clothing away for her
    B. tolerate the situation
    C. inspire her to be neat
    D. lecture her

30. A two-year-old child that refuses to eat lunch should

    A. be forced to eat
    B. be appeased
    C. not be forced to eat and the food should be removed without comment after a reasonable time has passed
    D. be scolded

31. Thumbsucking should be eliminated by

    A. satisfying the physical and emotional needs
    B. mechanical restraints
    C. applying distasteful compounds
    D. punishment

32. When Susan, a five-year-old, delights in telling fantastic stories, she should be

    A. punished   B. psychoanalyzed
    C. ignored   D. ridiculed

33. For 12-year-old children, an allowance

    A. may be used as a training device
    B. should be provided
    C. encourages a distorted sense of values
    D. provides a means of disciplinary control

34. Lefthandedness

    A. is an inherited trait   B. should be corrected
    C. indicates a shortcoming   D. is a conditioned reflex

35. To reduce fears in children, parents should

    A. give affection
    B. lecture them
    C. shield them
    D. provide safeguards

36. When a new baby is expected, to encourage a sense of belonging, older children should be allowed

    A. to anticipate another playmate
    B. no knowledge of the new baby
    C. to know but not talk about the new baby
    D. to share in the preparations

37. To ease an older child's adjustment to a new baby in the home, it is BEST to

    A. assure him that he is loved equally with the baby
    B. bolster his ego by reminding him of his baby days
    C. explain his responsibilities in helping to care for the new baby
    D. give him full attention when mother first arrives home with the new baby

38. Food cooked to suit the taste of an adult often proves to be unpleasant to a child because

    A. the child has a keener sense of taste than an adult has
    B. a child needs to be protected from eating foods he is not able to digest
    C. such foods are indigestible for him
    D. he needs to be taught to eat everything

39. In general, the _____ child will grow up to be most liberal.

    A. youngest
    B. middle
    C. oldest
    D. one cannot determine

40. In general, the _____ child will grow up to be most rigid.

    A. youngest
    B. middle
    C. oldest
    D. one cannot determine

KEY (CORRECT ANSWERS)

1. D	11. B	21. D	31. A
2. B	12. A	22. D	32. C
3. D	13. C	23. D	33. A
4. B	14. B	24. B	34. A
5. A	15. A	25. C	35. A
6. B	16. A	26. A	36. D
7. B	17. D	27. A	37. D
8. C	18. C	28. C	38. A
9. C	19. A	29. C	39. A
10. B	20. B	30. C	40. C

TEST 2

DIRECTIONS: Each question or incomplete statement is followed by several suggested answers or completions. Select the one that BEST answers the question or completes the statement. *PRINT THE LETTER OF THE CORRECT ANSWER IN THE SPACE AT THE RIGHT.*

1. For a child, the REAL purpose of play is to

    A. keep busy
    B. provide exercise
    C. provide self-expression
    D. discover abilities

2. Making a simple doll of yarn is a creative play experience enjoyed by the

    A. 3-year-old girl
    B. 4-5-year-old girl
    C. 4-5-year-old child
    D. 3-year-old child

3. An ideal kind of play for the child before meals and before bedtime is

    A. dramatic play
    B. quiet amusements
    C. construction play
    D. neighborhood games

4. To encourage good behavior in children, one should use

    A. candy rewards
    B. punishment for mistakes
    C. reasoning
    D. praise and approval for good behavior

5. A toy suitable for a child from infancy to two years of age should be

    A. free of sharp corners
    B. small things to climb on
    C. colored crayons
    D. easily broken

6. A child usually laces his own shoes at the age of _____ years.

    A. 3   B. 4   C. 5   D. 6

7. Girls' interest in clothes reaches its peak at about _____ years of age.

    A. 10   B. 12   C. 14   D. 16

8. In a child's speech development, his grammatical usage is reasonably accurate by the age of _____ years.

    A. 5   B. 3   C. 7   D. 9

9. A child should be able to pedal a tricycle at _____ year(s).

    A. 1   B. 2   C. 3   D. 4

10. The BEST antidote for jealousy in a child is to

    A. point out his defects to him
    B. extend love, overtly
    C. present an older sibling as a model
    D. fawn on a younger sibling

11. Books for the pre-school child should deal with

    A. science
    B. songs and games
    C. adventure
    D. everyday activities

12. Five-year olds enjoy kindergarten because they have

    A. ability to communicate
    B. capacity to move about
    C. receptiveness to new ideas
    D. developed a desire for sociability

13. A toy suitable for a two-year-old child is a(n)

    A. tinker toy
    B. erector set
    C. Punch and Judy puppet
    D. push-pull toy

14. Of the following, the MOST effective in training a child in obedience is

    A. consistency
    B. attention to comfort
    C. a firm, loud voice
    D. punishment for failure

15. Self-consciousness is a form of

    A. egotism   B. altruism   C. stoicism   D. pedantism

16. In young children, fear is MOST frequently accompanied by

    A. emotional shock
    B. screaming
    C. hiding
    D. investigating

17. In general, of the following, the factor which is MOST important in the development of emotional stability in children is

    A. adequate toys and playmates
    B. complete freedom of choice
    C. strict discipline
    D. happy family life

18. The drinking of coffee and carbonated drinks by children is discouraged MAINLY because these drinks

    A. are stimulants
    B. increase calorie intake
    C. are substituted by children for essential foods
    D. disturb the child's digestive system

19. Among the following statements concerning child feeding, the FALLACIOUS statement is:

    A. Hunger is the chief stimulus to willingness to eat
    B. Given free choice, children will choose a sound diet from a selection of foods
    C. Given free choice, children usually select a high carbohydrate diet washed down with palatable liquids
    D. Forcing usually results in stubborn refusal to eat

20. Stuttering in children is USUALLY associated with

    A. vitamin deficiency
    B. mental deficiency
    C. emotional conflict
    D. imitation of other stutterers

21. A child's tendency to pattern after his parents is known as

    A. identification   B. projection
    C. compensation   D. substitution

22. MOST educators agree that righthandedness should be

    A. disregarded if the child indicates a preference for the left hand
    B. forced
    C. encouraged in all actions
    D. encouraged for writing only

23. Parents should provide opportunities to habituate control of small muscles of the arms when the child

    A. eats solid food
    B. makes an effort to feed himself
    C. eats in restaurants
    D. attends school

24. Concerning a six-year-old child, parents who insist on absolute perfection may

    A. hamper future accomplishments
    B. encourage good habits
    C. increase mutual love
    D. destroy imitative performance

25. The mother of a family should engage in social activities outside the home because they will

    A. prepare her for earning a living should necessity arise
    B. help her to *grow* with her husband
    C. provide a means of solving the children's problems
    D. broaden her own viewpoints and continue development of her own personality

26. The BEST method of managing family finances is for the breadwinner to

    A. dole out the money when it is needed
    B. turn over all control to the spouse
    C. provide an allowance for each member of the family to use as he pleases
    D. plan cooperatively with the entire family

27. The home can BEST benefit the mental health of its members through

    A. development of attitudes which result in appropriate emotional expression
    B. an elementary knowledge of psychiatry
    C. a check on the psychosomatics of the older members
    D. regular physical check-ups

28. Toilet training should be

    A. started early
    B. geared to the child's ability
    C. based on age
    D. introduced promptly in a firm businesslike manner

29. When training a child in the use of his hands, one may avoid emotional tensions in the child by remembering that

    A. during the first few months, babies are ambidextrous
    B. it is a simple matter to change from the use of the left to the right hand
    C. it is a risky business to try to change from the use of the left to the right hand if the left has been established as the dominant one
    D. feelings of insecurity result if a child is allowed to develop lefthandedness

30. When a child expresses fear of darkness on retiring, the BEST procedure is to

    A. make light of his fears
    B. compel him to accept the darkness
    C. provide a dim light
    D. shame him for his fears

31. Studies comparing the desirability of feeding to premature infants formulas warmed to body temperature and those given directly on removal from the refrigerator show

    A. no significant difference
    B. disturbed sleep following intake of cold formula
    C. regurgitation following intake of cold formula
    D. slower weight gain with cold feeding

32. An envelope-type wrap covering a baby's hands and feet, as well as his body, is called a

    A. bunting   B. crawler   C. Gertrude   D. sacque

33. The water for the baby's bath should be _____ °F.

    A. 90   B. 95   C. 100   D. 105

34. At the end of one year, the weight of an infant in relation to its birth weight should be

    A. an increase of 12 ounces monthly
    B. double
    C. 20 pounds more
    D. triple

35. Breastfeeding

    A. is unimportant
    B. is a drain on the mother
    C. increases infant development
    D. provides temporary immunity

36. Non-conforming young children should be

   A. observed and trained while they are young
   B. permitted to outgrow their undesirable traits by themselves
   C. punished at rare intervals
   D. the subject of discussion between members of the family circle without others being present

37. A growing child should NOT drink coffee because it

   A. acts as a stimulant
   B. is habit-forming
   C. reduces milk intake
   D. spoils the appetite

38. An underweight child should be fed

   A. more bread
   B. greater quantities of all foods eaten
   C. starchy desserts
   D. fatty meat cuts

39. Anorexia is BEST treated by

   A. peer pressure
   B. parents
   C. school counseling
   D. medical intervention

40. Personality development is principally affected by

   A. genetics
   B. social experiences
   C. cultural background
   D. school

KEY (CORRECT ANSWERS)

1. C	11. D	21. A	31. A
2. C	12. D	22. A	32. A
3. B	13. D	23. B	33. C
4. D	14. A	24. A	34. D
5. A	15. A	25. D	35. C
6. C	16. C	26. D	36. A
7. C	17. D	27. A	37. C
8. A	18. C	28. B	38. B
9. C	19. B	29. C	39. D
10. B	20. C	30. C	40. A

EXAMINATION SECTION
TEST 1

DIRECTIONS: Each question or incomplete statement is followed by several suggested answers or completions. Select the one that BEST answers the question or completes the statement. *PRINT THE LETTER OF THE CORRECT ANSWER IN THE SPACE AT THE RIGHT.*

1. In Freud's theory, the aspect of personality that operates according to the pleasure principle is called the 1.____

   A. id
   B. ego
   C. superego
   D. unconditioned stimulus

2. The soundness with which a test measures what it is intended to measure is referred to as its 2.____

   A. validity
   B. reliability
   C. positive correlation
   D. statistical significance

3. When two treatments combine to have an effect that is greater than the sum of the individual treatment effects, we say that there is a _____ effect. 3.____

   A. main
   B. synergistic
   C. teratogen
   D. developmental systems

4. According to psychologist Kurt Lewin, *There is nothing so practical as a good* 4.____

   A. fact
   B. theory
   C. assumption
   D. 5-cent cigar

5. A researcher designs a study in which he will give candy to one group of children for breakfast, and eggs and cereal to a second group. He then plans to test the children's physical endurance during gym class at 9:30 in the morning.
Regarding this study, we can say that the type of food is the 5.____

   A. control variable
   B. dependent variable
   C. independent variable
   D. sample

6. In Pavlov's classic experiments with dogs, the bell was the 6.____

   A. unconditioned stimulus
   B. conditioned stimulus
   C. unconditioned response
   D. conditioned response

7. The practice of rooming-in allows the 7.____

   A. father to stay in the hospital room overnight
   B. hospital to double-up on rooms to save costs
   C. mother to stay at home to have the baby
   D. baby to be with the mother whenever the mother wishes

8. Which of the following is a statement fundamental to social learning theory? 8.____

   A. Many behaviors are learned gradually through shaping.
   B. Many behaviors are learned quickly through observation and imitation (modelling).
   C. The frequency of a desired behavior is affected by rewards contingent on the behavior.
   D. Knowledge is constructed as a result of interaction between the individual and the environment.

9. The belief that racial mixing results in inferior offspring is contradicted by the idea of

    A. paradigms
    B. critical periods
    C. hybrid vigor
    D. natural selection

10. Betty Rubin's newborn snuggles near his mom's breast and turns his head several times to find a good nursing position. Just then the phone rings loudly and he startles, throws his arms out and loses his comfortable position. Which two reflexes are illustrated in order of appearance?

    A. Babinski and Moro
    B. Rooting and Moro
    C. Rooting and Babinski
    D. Moro and Babinski

11. When looking at theories and applying them, they are NOT

    A. things that evolve over time
    B. facts
    C. systematic and organized assumptions
    D. affected by the theorist's social context

12. One reason for having a control group in an experimental study is to

    A. keep the children in the experimental group from controlling the outcome
    B. check to see if events external to the study made the experimental group score high or low
    C. see what happens to children who are initially different from the control group
    D. make the experiment a case study

13. A limited time period when rapid development takes place in an organ, a part of the body, or a behavior is referred to as a(n)

    A. age of viability
    B. developmental pull
    C. critical period
    D. pseudodevelopmental phase

14. Mrs. Jann says her new baby wants to learn things just because they are interesting. Who would agree with her?

    A. Freud
    B. Skinner
    C. Watson
    D. Piaget

15. Every gene is a sequence of

    A. somatic cells
    B. trophoblasts
    C. DMA
    D. chorionics

16. An individual's tendency to discount information that is not consistent with what he or she already believes is an example of

    A. negation bias
    B. confirmatory bias
    C. blind procedure
    D. construct validity

17. During the first half of the 20th century, there were a number of movements designed to improve humankind by eliminating, sterilizing, or forbidding marriage to individuals perceived to be inferior. These are classified as

    A. ego-defense
    B. classical conditioning
    C. social interactionist
    D. eugenics

18. Reflexes such as rooting, Babinski, Moro, and tonic neck

    A. develop slowly during the neonatal and infancy periods
    B. replace the voluntary movements made by infants at birth
    C. begin to appear after neonates are able to maintain a normal body temperature
    D. are typically replaced by voluntary behaviors during the first year of life

19. Piaget indicated that babies know about the world through their interactions with objects. He called this

    A. object reality
    B. object permanence
    C. sensorimotor intelligence
    D. state interaction

20. Which of the following statements is based on a *behavioral* view of child development?

    A. Children seek stimulation.
    B. You may play with your toys after you have cleaned up your room.
    C. Children need to work out their emotional conflicts through dramatic play.
    D. Leave her alone; she'll grow out of it.

21. Alcohol and cigarette smoke are examples of environmental agents that adversely affect prenatal development. They are called

    A. anoxias   B. perinatals
    C. surrogates   D. teratogens

22. Which of the following is an important focus in the development systems approach to child development?

    A. Mutual interaction throughout many levels of organization
    B. Neurological maturation
    C. Equilibration
    D. Progression from one stage to the next

23. Which of the following is NOT an example of a social biological effect?
    A

    A. child's exposure to high levels of lead resulting in a lowered IQ
    B. child born with fetal alcohol syndrome
    C. child who develops a fear of dogs after being bitten
    D. man living near Chernobyl whose sperm have chromosomal damage

24. A child who is learning soccer skills might be guided through the zone of proximal development by

    A. having the child practice with a more skilled peer
    B. receiving a reinforcement for each skill level mastered
    C. exposure to unconditioned stimuli
    D. shaping successive approximations to the target behavior

25. Do infants who sleep separately from their mothers grow up to be more independent than those who sleep with their mothers?

   A. Yes
   B. No
   C. There is no research on this
   D. There is no definitive answer according to research done

KEY (CORRECT ANSWERS)

1.	A	11.	B
2.	A	12.	B
3.	B	13.	C
4.	B	14.	D
5.	C	15.	C
6.	B	16.	B
7.	D	17.	D
8.	B	18.	D
9.	C	19.	C
10.	B	20.	B

21. D
22. A
23. C
24. A
25. D

TEST 2

DIRECTIONS: Each question or incomplete statement is followed by several suggested answers or completions. Select the one that BEST answers the question or completes the statement. *PRINT THE LETTER OF THE CORRECT ANSWER IN THE SPACE AT THE RIGHT.*

1. Depth perception is

   A. formed from concepts
   B. learned by habituation
   C. innate
   D. modeled from parents

   1.____

2. Grammatical errors are common in the language of preschoolers. Which of the following is appropriate advice for how to handle grammatical errors?

   A. Use a direct approach by saying *No,* then telling them how they should say the sentence
   B. With each error, ask a question about what the child said, using the correct use of the word in the question
   C. Say, *Please try saying that sentence again*
   D. Listen for content and use the correct grammar in conversational responses to the child

   2.____

3. The Chess and Thomas longitudinal study of easy, difficult, and slow-to-warm-up children suggests that the _____ is critical for successful child rearing.

   A. goodness-of-fit between child temperament and parental interaction styles
   B. genetic temperament of the child matters more than the initial parenting style
   C. initial parenting style matters more than the early temperament of the child
   D. child's genetics and peer group

   3.____

4. Preschooler Seth Thomas is counting a dozen blocks on the table. He touches them all, some twice, and ends up with a count of 15. What kind of counting error is he making?

   A. Coordination
   B. Hierarchical
   C. Partitioning
   D. Tagging

   4.____

5. Which of the following is NOT a good example of functional autonomy?

   A. Brushing your teeth
   B. Good manners
   C. Bulimia
   D. Breathing

   5.____

6. Which of the following is most likely to promote locomotor development in 4-month-old infants?

   A. Placing them in a stomach-down prone position on the floor
   B. Laying them on their backs and encouraging spontaneous leg exercises
   C. Providing lots of pillows to permit climbing and more upright positioning
   D. Stimulating after 6 months since development isn't facilitated until then

   6.____

7. The degree to which a 9-month-old exhibits stranger anxiety can be reduced by

   A. the mother being in constant contact with her baby
   B. the child's inability to crawl or walk away
   C. social referencing
   D. social games

   7.____

8. According to a research study, when mothers brought their babies in for a doctor's examination, it was found that the group of mothers who stood closest to their babies had more early contact with their children. It is difficult to argue that this means that these mothers had bonded better with their children because the outcome measure lacks _____ validity.

   A. predictive
   B. face
   C. external
   D. internal

9. Which of the following are characteristics of infant-directed or child-directed speech (CDS)?

   A. More narrow pitch range
   B. Less contrast between high and low pitches
   C. Longer pauses between words
   D. All of the above

10. According to analysis of Maccoby's study on infants' babbling, does babbling relate to or predict later intelligence?

    A. *Yes*, for boys only
    B. *Yes*, for girls only
    C. *Yes*, for both boys and girls
    D. *No*; when boys and girls are separated, there is no relation

11. Which of the following is the most noticeable change in appearance during the preschool years?

    A. Protruding stomach
    B. Rapid growth of legs and trunk
    C. Fast growth in height
    D. Weight gained faster than during year one

12. During the preschool years, there are many changes in motor development. Which of the following is NOT an accurate statement about motor development changes?

    A. Fine motor development of the fingers allows marked improvement in coloring, cutting, and pasting.
    B. Because their center of gravity moves up, they are more coordinated in climbing and jumping.
    C. Jumping ability improves markedly in part due to thrusting their arms forward rather than *winging* their arms in a jump.
    D. In climbing ladders and jungle gyms, there is a change from marked-time climbing to alternating feet.

13. Which of the following was found to be a productive way to overcome attachment difficulties between mothers and babies during the first year of life?

    A. Trying to get the baby to imitate the mother's actions
    B. Soliciting the baby's attention when he looked away
    C. Teaching the mother to choose appropriate responses to the baby's signals
    D. Teaching the mother to plan a regular schedule of activities in order to establish a routine with the infant

14. In number conservation tasks, most preschoolers judge which row has more objects by

   A. the length of the row
   B. counting the objects in the display
   C. making another row that is identical to the first and counting objects as they make the second row
   D. compensation

15. By 6 years of age, when most children enter first grade, their vocabularies range from about _____ words.

   A. 3,000-6,000
   B. 7,000-9,000
   C. 10,000-14,000
   D. 15,000-20,000

16. Baby Shemirah now has the ability to imagine actions in her head. Piaget would say that this ability allows a strong concept of

   A. object permanence
   B. imagination
   C. habituation
   D. fixation

17. A significantly slower than average rate of growth that is due to feeding and caregiving problems rather than to disease or heredity is termed

   A. encropresis
   B. failure-to-thrive
   C. slow-growth syndrome
   D. maturational lag

18. Two-month-old baby Watson looks longer at his own mother than he does at the occasional sitter, visiting grandma, or the bookmobile delivery woman. This recognition is based upon his mother's

   A. facial features
   B. hairline
   C. eye contact
   D. voice cues

19. At age 11 months, Missy started saying *da-da* rather than her usual *dadadada*. According to developmental linguists, she is now

   A. overextending
   B. babbling
   C. modifying
   D. using a protoword

20. Peter and his younger sister Sally were playing *house,* Peter told Sally to set the table while he cooked the turkey, showing her how to count the forks and napkins. Then he asked her to think of a good desert.
    Peter is _____ his sister's pretend play abilities.

   A. categorizing
   B. scaffolding
   C. modeling
   D. decentrizing

21. Jill can't take another point of view and tells you what the child sitting on the other side of the mountain can see. Piaget would say that she is

   A. hierarchical
   B. self-centered
   C. identity-bound
   D. egocentric

22. Many 3-year-old children were quite frightened by the dinosaur movie, JURASSIC PARK. The reason is that younger children

    A. can't centrate on film
    B. can't distinguish appearance from reality
    C. have highly tuned emotional systems
    D. have too much imagination

23. Which of the following is supported by research on infant and toddler development?

    A. The weight of the brain's cortex is unaffected by environmental factors.
    B. It is fairly easy to separate the effects of malnourishment and stimulation deprivation.
    C. About 10% of the adult's brain weight develops during the first two years.
    D. A stimulating environment can produce more growth of brain cells.

24. Selma is 3 years old. Her dad has read TEDDY BEAR, TEDDY BEAR to her many times. Now Selma can *read* it aloud with inflection, even though she isn't actually reading the words. Selma is a(n) _____ reader.

    A. beginning   B. coded
    C. emergent   D. syllabic

25. Which of the following is true concerning hearing problems in infants?

    A. It is difficult for infants to learn sign language.
    B. When deaf children learn sign language, they learn it at a slower rate than hearing children learn oral language.
    C. If infants make vocal sounds, they must be able to hear them.
    D. Infants learning sign language babble in sign just as hearing infants babble orally.

KEY (CORRECT ANSWERS)

1. C
2. D
3. A
4. C
5. D

6. A
7. C
8. B
9. C
10. B

11. B
12. B
13. C
14. A
15. C

16. A
17. B
18. B
19. D
20. B

21. D
22. B
23. D
24. C
25. D

TEST 3

DIRECTIONS: Each question or incomplete statement is followed by several suggested answers or completions. Select the one that BEST answers the question or completes the statement. *PRINT THE LETTER OF THE CORRECT ANSWER IN THE SPACE AT THE RIGHT.*

1. Kohlberg called the first level of moral development *preconventional.* At this level, children make moral decisions

    A. based on what is expected of them by society
    B. based on a simple set of philosophical principles
    C. on the basis of self-interest
    D. on the basis of living up to what close family members expect of them

2. The ability to attend to the form rather than the meaning of language is called

    A. phonological awareness
    B. metalinguistic awareness
    C. multisyllabic interpretations
    D. word boundary interpretations

3. Emotions can have positive or negative natures. This is called the

    A. target   B. valence   C. surrogate   D. polarity

4. Which of the following illustrates the secular growth trend?

    A. April is an Olympic champion in running and hasn't begun her menstrual period, even at age 15.
    B. June is very uncomfortable with her transition to adulthood based mainly on her individual perceptions.
    C. August is beginning her menstrual period at age 11, and her great-grandmother, who didn't begin until 15, is quite concerned.
    D. October is not faring very well in academics or social situations and her doctor wants her checked for secondary characteristics.

5. Carl has not seen the word *unbending* before, but he knows what *bending* means. Since he also understands *un*, he will be able to figure out what *unbending* means by

    A. understanding the word from its grammatical structure
    B. inferring word meaning from morphological knowledge
    C. learning from the suffix information
    D. getting the meaning from context

6. When Maria finally realizes that she will always be a girl, even if she cuts her hair or changes her clothes, we say she has achieved

    A. gender identity   B. gender constancy
    C. gender typing   D. sex-role structure

7. Why does Piaget label the thinking of school-age children as *concrete operational*?

    A. As long as they can see what they are talking about, or are familiar with it, they can think logically.
    B. While they cannot think abstractly, they can cement abstract ideas together if they make sense.
    C. Since the structure is basic or concrete, the thinking process can only be basic.
    D. They can juggle variables and contemplate possibilities about situations that exist only in their minds.

8. In the 3-kinds-of-memory-store model, which memory is our *working memory*?

    A. Sensory
    B. Long-term
    C. Short-term
    D. Intermediate

9. Carrie, a third grade girl, according to the research on beliefs and expectations is most likely to

    A. respond to failure by increasing her efforts
    B. believe that when she fails, she can expect more reinforcement from her teacher
    C. attribute failure to a lack of ability
    D. attribute her poor performance to nonintellectual aspects of her work

10. Race was examined as a risk factor in Sameroff's study because

    A. research has demonstrated that children from different races vary in their risk-taking behavior
    B. race is related to many negative outcomes in our society, even if it does not cause them
    C. minority children mature earlier, which puts them at risk
    D. experiments have demonstrated a causal relationship between race and cognitive performance

11. In regard to socialization and moral development, _____ is the process whereby adult values are adopted as the child's own, and _____ explains why the child adopts, the characteristics of the same-sex parent.

    A. social responsiveness; proximity seeking
    B. proximity seeking; social responsiveness
    C. identification; internalization
    D. internalization; identification

12. Cleo's dad decided to ignore Cleo's whining about not wanting to go to bed. Eventually she stopped whining. One night she smiled as she was putting on her pajamas, and her dad said, *My, I do like to see those nice bedtime smiles.* Cleo became happier about bedtime.
    Her clever dad first used a(n) _____ procedure, then a(n) _____ procedure.

    A. social cognition; reinforcement
    B. extinction; reinforcement
    C. extinction; exhortation
    D. social cognition; exhortation

13. Sternberg's triarchic theory of intelligence differentiates between which three aspects of mental ability?   13.____

    A. Verbal, quantitative, analytical
    B. Analytical, creative, practical
    C. Logical-mathematical, bodily-kinesthetic, interpersonal
    D. Memory, convergent, divergent

14. _____ are the primary engines of development,   14.____

    A. Chaos and individualism   B. Continuity and change
    C. Proximal processes   D. Peer groups

15. What is the level of intelligence for most ADHD children?   15.____

    A. Above normal   B. Normal
    C. Below normal   D. No data available

16. Which of the following best describes brain growth during the school-age years?   16.____

    A. Brain weight equals adult levels by age 6.
    B. Brain myelination is complete by age 7.
    C. Brain lateralization begins at age 6.
    D. The head grows quickly during the school-age years.

17. Sally is going through tremendous physical changes and is increasing in height and weight very quickly. However, she has not yet reached menarche. What term do we give to this period of development?   17.____

    A. Puberty   B. Juvenescence
    C. Pubescence   D. Presexagesimal

18. Changes that occurred in diary recordings from the late 19th century to the early 20th century were from   18.____

    I. no explicit sexual content in entries in the 19th century to entries discussing heterosexual and homosexual behaviors in the 20th century
    II. strong family loyalty apparent in entries in the 19th century to disregard for parents and thoughts of running away in the 20th century
    III. entries planning to make alterations in one's character in the 19th century to plans to make alterations in one's outer appearances in the 20th century

    The CORRECT answer is:

    A. I only   B. II only   C. I, III   D. I, II, III

19. Over the course of this century, the ratio of youths to adults has   19.____

    A. steadily increased
    B. steadily decreased
    C. both decreased and increased
    D. mirrored the secular growth trend

20. Which of the following is a secondary sex characteristic?   20.____

    A. Ovulation   B. Menstruation
    C. Axillary hair   D. Muscle development

21. Some data shows that little girls don't imitate Batman and Power Rangers nearly as much as little boys do. According to Bandura, this occurs because

    A. girls are innately less aggressive
    B. boys have more imagination
    C. girls don't perceive themselves as similar to the models
    D. boys don't want to be perceived as *sissies*

22. Sue's preschool teacher said to her, *You're spending so much time on those drawings, and they are so colorful! Won't they look niee on the art wall!* Sue sees herself as an artist, and returns to the painting area every day. Her teacher has used

    A. verbal prompting   B. response cost
    C. positive attribution   D. social cognizing

23. Studies of children who have been exposed to violence show all but one of the following:

    A. Exposure to violence decreases children's future orientation
    B. Real news on television helps children to understand that violence is not a major threat
    C. Children's confidence is declining for believing that adults can protect them from violence
    D. Children are becoming desensitive to violence

24. What does current research point to as the primary problem in dyslexia?

    A. Language processing   B. Vision problems
    C. Visual-motor problems   D. Low intelligence

25. Arnold Sameroff's study of the accumulation of risk factors shows that

    A. each accumulation of an additional risk factor in a child's environment was related to an equal decrease in the child's later IQ
    B. categorical programs are likely to be the most successful at dealing with the accumulation of risk factors
    C. some risk factors put a child at much greater risk for a decreased IQ than others
    D. children with one or two risk factors had only slightly lower later IQs than those with no risk factors

KEY (CORRECT ANSWERS)

1. C
2. B
3. B
4. C
5. B

6. B
7. A
8. C
9. C
10. B

11. D
12. B
13. B
14. C
15. B

16. A
17. C
18. C
19. C
20. C

21. C
22. C
23. B
24. A
25. D

EXAMINATION SECTION
TEST 1

DIRECTIONS: Each question or incomplete statement is followed by several suggested answers or completions. Select the one that BEST answers the question or completes the statement. *PRINT THE LETTER OF THE CORRECT ANSWER IN THE SPACE AT THE RIGHT.*

1. According to psychoanalytic theory, the part of the personality which is in closest contact with reality is the

    A. id
    B. superego
    C. libido
    D. ego

    1.____

2. An individual who gives socially acceptable reasons for his behavior, either verbally, by thought, or conduct, is adjusting through the use of

    A. rationalization
    B. sublimation
    C. retrogression
    D. displacement

    2.____

3. Of the following statements, the MOST nearly correct one regarding the rate of mental growth is that

    A. there is a deceleration of the rate of growth with age
    B. there is an increase in the rate of growth with age
    C. mental growth is constant throughout the period of childhood
    D. mental growth is constant during adulthood

    3.____

4. In early childhood, the individual tends to pattern himself on or to identify himself MOST generally with

    A. glamorous or romantic figures
    B. age contemporaries
    C. characters in movies or on TV
    D. parents or parent substitutes

    4.____

5. With respect to physical growth, superior children as compared with children of average intelligence are

    A. slightly inferior
    B. above average
    C. slightly superior
    D. markedly inferior

    5.____

6. A candidate in an examination says, "I passed the written and the performance tests, but they failed me in the interview." The mechanism of personality defense which he is employing is

    A. compensation
    B. sublimation
    C. identification
    D. projection

    6.____

7. The psychological forces or needs that influence human behavior are labeled

    A. extrasensory
    B. generalized
    C. intrinsic
    D. extrinsic

    7.____

8. Reactions of nail biting, grimacing, clawing, spitting, etc. in a fourth-grade child are usually considered symptomatic evidence of

    A. low intelligence
    B. psychological conflict
    C. hypothyroidism
    D. nervousness

    8.____

9. The greatest "social distance" in boy-girl relationships has been found to be during the ages

   A. 13 to 17 years
   B. 9 to 13 years
   C. 5 to 9 years
   D. 2 to 5 years

10. According to available findings, the effect of deprivation of affection on intellectual development is MOST likely to appear in a curtailment of the

    A. speed of learning even when the task is rather simple
    B. ability to memorize new material
    C. ability to retain material, once it has been learned
    D. ability to conceptualize

11. Of the following, the one which would MOST likely indicate faulty emotional development in a girl of six is

    A. striving for perfection in all her work
    B. stronger liking for music than other school work
    C. little interest in doll play
    D. reluctance to engage in competitive sports

12. When a six-year-old child violates the standards of conduct of the group, the teacher should

    A. criticize him in the presence of the group
    B. accept his behavior as the expression of a deep need
    C. support him in order to alleviate his guilt feelings
    D. discourage his behavior by showing why it is wrong

13. A shy child is MOST likely to be fairly well adjusted if he has

    A. clearly defined interests
    B. marked intellectual ability
    C. obvious physical handicaps
    D. outstanding artistic talent

14. A kindergarten child shows habitual reluctance to undertake a new activity. This is BEST interpreted as evidence of

    A. an inability to cope with adult authority
    B. a general attitude of insecurity
    C. a specific fear conditioned in infancy
    D. a persevering and independent attitude

15. For a four-year-old child, the events of the present are

    A. less vivid than those of the past
    B. less vivid than those of the future
    C. more vivid than those of the past or future
    D. as vivid as those of the past or future

16. The "ideal self" represents what an individual

    A. believes he ought to be
    B. believes others ought to be
    C. knows he can be
    D. knows he cannot be

17. Girls generally prefer groups of girls and boys prefer groups of boys during

    A. early childhood   B. latency
    C. pre-adolescence   D. adolescence

18. The rate and pattern of early motor development are largely determined by

    A. experience   B. learning
    C. maturation   D. training

19. Which of the following books describes how parents and other adults can help youngsters overcome problems of an urban environment?

    A. YOUR ADOLESCENT, L. K. and Mary Frank
    B. STUDIES IN ADOLESCENCE, Robert E. Grinder
    C. IN DEFENSE OF YOUTH, by Earl C. Kelley
    D. THE AMERICAN TEENAGER, by H.H. Remmers and D.H. Radler

20. When a person has gained some insight into his own emotional behavior, usually following resolution of an acute conflict, we often describe him as having increased his range of

    A. emotional repression   B. affective mobility
    C. understanding   D. clinical synapses

21. Sibling rivalry is the term used to describe the competitive feeling between two or more individuals who

    A. are in the same school grade
    B. are children of the same parents
    C. have similar goals of achievement
    D. are in the same chronological age group

22. The mental mechanism of minimizing one's own faults and deficiencies by criticizing and blaming others is known as

    A. compensation   B. rationalization
    C. transference   D. projection

23. Etiology is concerned primarily with

    A. symptomology   B. racial origin
    C. causation   D. language facility

24. Syndrome is BEST defined as a

    A. form of obsession in which the subject sees himself as someone else
    B. form of neurosis in which the subject constantly compares himself with others
    C. cardiac condition which has no apparent organic basis
    D. constellation of symptoms which characteristically occur together in a specific ailment

4 (#1)

25. Girls tend to be superior to boys of the same age in

   A. linguistic fluency
   B. speed of reaction time
   C. arithmetical reasoning
   D. most forms of perception

26. Of the following, a major recreational activity common to both 10- and 15-year-old boys and girls is

   A. going to the movies
   B. riding a bicycle
   C. watching athletic sports
   D. social dancing

27. In general, juvenile fiction comprises the major part of the reading choices of

   A. girls between 9 and 13
   B. boys of all ages
   C. girls of all ages
   D. boys between 12 and 16

28. The behavior of the typical adolescent is BEST described as characteristically

   A. stubborn and willful, showing disregard for strictures of family and society
   B. inconsistent, alternating between childish and adult reactions
   C. irresponsible, exhibiting lack of judgment and poor taste
   D. individualistic, reflecting indifference to approval from parents and peers

29. Of the following observed behavior symptoms, the one which may BEST be described as "regression" is the pupil's

   A. use of infantile speech and verbal expressions
   B. thrusting aside of present desires in order to avoid conflict in a direct solution of a problem
   C. attempt to dominate every situation in which he finds himself
   D. evasion of possible failure by selecting an easier goal

30. UNDERSTANDING GROUP BEHAVIOR OF BOYS AND GIRLS was written by

   A. Helen H. Jennings
   B. Ruth Cunningham
   C. Jane Waters
   D. Alice V. Crow

31. When we compare young children and adolescents with respect to the relative effectiveness of distributed and concentrated practice as a learning technique, we find that

   A. young children learn better by distributed practice; adolescents by concentrated practice
   B. young children learn better by concentrated practice; adolescents by distributed practice
   C. both young children and adolescents learn better by concentrated practice
   D. both young children and adolescents learn better by distributed practice

32. Research has demonstrated that there is an increase in racial prejudice during adolescence. Of the following, the factor that contributes MOST significantly to this increase is

A. dislike for deviants from norms of social groups
B. influence of parental opinion
C. segregation of groups in school and community
D. fear of economic pressure from minority groups

33. Of the following teachers, the one MOST liked by the largest number of junior high school pupils is the one who

   A. sets easily attainable standards
   B. demonstrates a high level of intellectual competence
   C. maintains an impersonal, objective attitude
   D. is sympathetic

33.____

34. Of the following, the behavior which would be considered MOST indicative of potential or actual maladjustment in a junior high school boy is

   A. treating his classmates to sodas in an attempt to buy their votes in a school election
   B. spending his entire allowance each week on science fiction paperbacks
   C. finding fault with the work of his classmates
   D. failing to take care of school property

34.____

35. The proportion of TREATED juvenile delinquents who exhibit subsequent histories of failure to adjust to society is about

   A. 5%   B. 25%   C. 45%   D. 65%

35.____

36. Current evidence and thinking on the causative factors in juvenile delinquency support the view that

   A. social factors are more basic than psychological factor
   B. psychological factors are more basic than social factor
   C. psychological factors and social factors are of about equal importance
   D. physiological factors are more important than either social or psychological factors

36.____

37. Studies involving the relative mental abilities of delinquent and non-delinquent children have generally

   A. shown that there are no significant differences between them
   B. shown that delinquent children are slightly but significantly brighter than non-delinquents
   C. shown that non-delinquent children are somewhat brighter than delinquent children
   D. been about evenly divided some finding the delinquent children brighter, others finding mental superiority for non-delinquents

37.____

38. Separation of the infant from his mother can be a traumatic experience. The amount of emotional damage to the infant and the consequent effects on his personality depend MAINLY on the

   A. quality and consistency of the substitute mothering he receives
   B. reasons for and duration of the separation
   C. kind of preparation for separation the infant receives
   D. degree of the mother's acceptance of the placement

38.____

39. Research studies of language development in young children have shown that

    A. the multiple mothering of children in a large family delays language development
    B. language delay in otherwise normal children is usually related to inadequate language stimulation
    C. language delay is always associated with slow motor development
    D. children are usually slow in learning to talk when more than one language is spoken in the home

40. The two MOST important influences on the cultural development of a seven-year-old child are the

    A. home and peer group   B. school and peer group
    C. home and school   D. home and church

41. In our culture, a child gains his sense of identity MAINLY from

    A. knowledge about and experience with his parents and extended family
    B. association with members of his own ethnic group
    C. a study of the historical and ethnic factors in this culture
    D. association with his peers

42. Of the following, the MOST important influence on the personality development of a child during the first year is the

    A. family as a whole
    B. mother
    C. way his siblings react to him
    D. relationship between the parents

43. Of the following, the term which is generally applied to the situation in which an infant in foster care has insufficient interaction with a substitute mother is

    A. maternal rejection   B. mothering complex
    C. maternal deprivation   D. interaction deficiency

44. The normal four-year-old child should be expected to

    A. cut her meat with a knife
    B. bathe herself without help
    C. care for herself at the toilet
    D. tell time to the nearest quarter hour

45. It is usually not a good idea to take a child under the age of five to a movie that may frighten him MAINLY because young children cannot

    A. appreciate a cultural experience
    B. behave themselves in a movie theater
    C. distinguish clearly between real life and make believe
    D. see movies without acting out what they see

46. The average five-year-old child spends the MAJOR part of his play time

    A. playing by himself
    B. watching other children play
    C. playing cooperatively with other children
    D. playing competitive games involving teams

47. A children's counselor faced with a question about sex from a six-year-old child in her group should

    A. tell the child she is too young to understand such things
    B. give the child as honest and simple an answer as possible
    C. realize that an older child must have told the six-year-old to ask that question
    D. answer the question in such a way as to discourage the child from asking any more questions about sex

48. Most studies of children's fears indicate that fears of the supernatural are MOST common among the

    A. pre-schoolers   B. latency-age group
    C. pre-adolescents   D. adolescents

49. The boy who trips on the leg of a chair and then accuses the chair is using the mechanism of

    A. rationalization   B. regression
    C. daydreaming   D. projection

50. Mild amounts of emotion, such as anxiety, irritation, and apprehension, tend to have which of the following influences on learning and performance?

    A. Integrative   B. Mildly disintegrative
    C. Disruptive   D. Relatively little influence

KEY (CORRECT ANSWERS)

1. D	11. A	21. B	31. D	41. A
2. A	12. D	22. D	32. A	42. B
3. A	13. A	23. C	33. D	43. C
4. D	14. B	24. D	34. C	44. C
5. C	15. C	25. A	35. B	45. C
6. D	16. A	26. A	36. B	46. C
7. C	17. B	27. A	37. C	47. B
8. B	18. C	28. B	38. A	48. B
9. B	19. C	29. A	39. B	49. D
10. D	20. B	30. B	40. C	50. A

TEST 2

DIRECTIONS: Each question or incomplete statement is followed by several suggested answers or completions. Select the one that BEST answers the question or completes the statement. *PRINT THE LETTER OF THE CORRECT ANSWER IN THE SPACE AT THE RIGHT.*

1. The process by which children take to themselves the values, the thinking, and the social behavior of their parents is known as

   A. projection
   B. identification
   C. denigration
   D. sublimation
   E. imitation

   1.____

2. An understanding of the family relationships of a youngster who presents a problem of under-achievement

   A. is worthwhile but not essential
   B. is important but not within the province of the teacher
   C. may reveal factors that have an important bearing on his problem
   D. is unlikely to be related to the difficulties the young person has with his school work
   E. is important but not within the province of the guidance counselor

   2.____

3. Which of the following is the MOST correct statement concerning puberty and physical maturity?

   A. Boys and girls who experience early puberty will achieve physical maturity and cease growing later than will the late maturers.
   B. Boys and girls who experience early puberty will achieve physical maturity and cease growing sooner than will the late maturers.
   C. Boys and girls who experience early puberty will achieve physical maturity and cease growing at approximately the same time as the late maturers.
   D. Boys and girls who experience early puberty will achieve physical maturity and cease growing in any standard pattern, together with the late maturers.
   E. None of the above.

   3.____

4. The MOST prominent difficulties of the middle years of childhood revolve around

   A. relations with peer groups
   B. parent-child relationships
   C. schooling and the ability to learn
   D. physical development
   E. emotional and spiritual development

   4.____

5. The MOST accurate statement concerning anxiety, of the following, is that anxiety is

   A. needed for the socialization process
   B. not needed for the socialization process
   C. less produced by "mental" punishment than by physical punishment
   D. of negligible effect in producing neurosis
   E. neutralized by feelings of guilt and inadequacy

   5.____

6. Most studies of children's fears indicate that fears of the supernatural are MOST common among the

   A. early childhood group
   B. latency-age group
   C. pre-teen group
   D. adolescents
   E. early childhood group and adolescents as contrasted with the pre-teen and latency-age groups

7. The boy who trips on the leg of a chair and then accuses the chair is using the mechanism of

   A. rationalization B. regression
   C. sublimation   D. projection
   E. delusion

8. Mild amounts of emotion, such as anxiety, irritation, and apprehension, tend to have which of the following influences on learning and performance?

   A. Integrative   B. Mildly disintegrative
   C. Disruptive   D. Integrative and segregative
   E. Disruptive and disintegrative

9. The "ideal self" represents what an individual

   A. believes he ought to be
   B. believes others ought to be
   C. knows he can be
   D. knows others can be
   E. believes he ought to be and can be

10. Girls generally prefer groups of girls AND boys prefer groups of boys during

    A. early childhood
    B. latency
    C. pre-adolescence
    D. adolescence
    E. early childhood and pre-adolescence

11. The rate and pattern of early motor development are largely determined by

    A. experience   B. learning
    C. maturation   D. training
    E. practice

12. Changes in cognitive behavior between childhood and adolescence are in the direction of greater

    A. understanding of abstractions
    B. reliance on concrete realities
    C. dependence on vicarious experiences
    D. emphasis on intuition
    E. collection of scattered peripheral details

13. Gesell refers to the child's development between the ages of six and ten as

    A. an ever-widening spiral
    B. a task phase
    C. a latency period
    D. a transitional interval
    E. an imitative stage

14. A defense mechanism defined as the adoption of an attitude opposite to one that precedes anxiety is

    A. sophistry
    B. reaction formation
    C. fantasy
    D. verification
    E. rationalization

15. Experiments with the reactions of varying age groups to snakes indicated that, in general, the greatest fear was exhibited by

    A. infants
    B. primary pupils
    C. latency-age children
    D. adolescents
    E. E. adults

16. As children get older, the differences in ability between the bright and the dull tend to

    A. become smaller
    B. become larger
    C. remain about the same
    D. vary in no set pattern
    E. become larger, level off, and then become smaller

17. Which one of the following descriptions is characteristic of the actively-rejected home?

    A. Parents show highly emotional attitude, warmth without understanding.
    B. Parents tend to use severe punishment only if irritated.
    C. Parents restrict child's independence with many rules and requirements.
    D. Child is expected to make his own decisions, although advice is unavailable.
    E. Parents are jealous of, and in active competition with, their children.

18. Homesickness is an example of which type of adjustment mechanism?

    A. Guilt
    B. Identification
    C. Reaction
    D. Sublimation
    E. Regression

19. Children below the age of 10 when asked to write on "The person I would like to be" most frequently want to vie with

    A. peers
    B. older siblings
    C. parents
    D. real or imaginary heroes
    E. teachers

20. When a child strikes out at a person who did not provoke the anger, the child is exhibiting

    A. depression
    B. retrogression
    C. compensation
    D. displaced aggression
    E. projection

21. Which of the following statements describes the effect upon intellectually gifted children of early school entrance and acceleration?

    A. It serves to delay their social development.
    B. It produces underachievers.
    C. It creates emotional problems.
    D. It leads to favorable and valuable results.
    E. It substantially affects the development of motor skills.

22. The psychological forces or needs that influence human behavior are labeled

    A. extrasensory
    B. extrinsic
    C. intrinsic
    D. generalized
    E. contingent

23. Reactions of nail biting, grimacing, clawing, spitting, etc. in a fourth-grade child are usually considered symptomatic evidence of

    A. anxiety
    B. dementia
    C. low intelligence
    D. hypothyroidism
    E. psychological conflict

24. An individual who gives socially acceptable reasons for his behavior, either verbally, by thought, or conduct, is adjusting through the use of

    A. rationalization
    B. displacement
    C. sublimation
    D. retrogression
    E. projection

25. Of the following statements, the MOST NEARLY correct one regarding the rate of mental growth is that

    A. there is a deceleration of the rate of growth with age
    B. mental growth is constant during adulthood
    C. mental growth is constant throughout the period of childhood
    D. there is an increase in the rate of growth with age
    E. the rate of mental growth increases and decreases in a standard pattern

26. In early childhood, the individual tends to pattern himself on or to identify himself MOST generally with

    A. glamorous or romantic figures
    B. age contemporaries
    C. characters in movies or on TV
    D. parents or parent substitutes
    E. older siblings

27. With respect to physical growth, mentally superior children as compared with children of average intelligence are

    A. markedly inferior
    B. slightly inferior
    C. slightly superior
    D. markedly superior
    E. about average

28. A candidate in an examination says, "I passed the written and the performance tests, but they failed me in the interview." The mechanism of personality defense which he is employing is

    A. compensation
    B. sublimation
    C. identification
    D. projection
    E. rationalization

29. The psychologist whose name is MOST often associated with the theory that the experience of birth has a profound influence on personality development and that an individual who has a slow, prolonged birth is likely to have a personality which fights, struggles and plunges is

    A. Horney
    B. Freud
    C. Sullivan
    D. Rank
    E. McDougall

30. Two different studies have suggested that children who will probably have lower I.Q.'s are those who have been reared in

    A. institutions
    B. broken homes
    C. foster homes
    D. upper class homes
    E. lower class homes

31. Studies of twins reared together indicate that the correlation coefficients of intelligence tests scores for identical twins lie in the range of

    A. .40-.55
    B. .65-.74
    C. .75-.79
    D. .80-.90
    E. .90-1.00

32. As a means of changing the current behavior pattern of an adolescent, which of the following forces will generally prove to be MOST potent? Disapproval of the behavior pattern by

    A. the adolescent's parents
    B. an adult he admires
    C. a group of his peers
    D. his classroom teacher
    E. older siblings

33. If the results of studies of boys' clubs are applicable to the school situation, one may expect the greatest amount of aggressive behavior to be noted in classes where the classroom climate may be described as

    A. permissive
    B. laissez-faire
    C. democratic
    D. autocratic
    E. unstructured

34. Of the following, the LEAST effective way of dealing with children's fears is

    A. explaining and reassuring
    B. helping the child to face the feared situation
    C. simply ignoring the child's fears
    D. setting examples of fearlessness
    E. removing the cause of fear from the child's environment

35. The age at which individuals cease to grow in intellectual ability is

    A. 13 years
    B. 16 years
    C. 21 years
    D. 35 years
    E. probably none of these

36. The theory that physical compensation for a feeling of physical or social inferiority is responsible for the development of a psychoneurosis is attributed to

    A. Adler
    B. Horney
    C. Freud
    D. Sullivan
    E. Jung

37. Which of the following terms refers to the maintenance of stability in the physiological functioning of the organism?

    A. functional autonomy
    B. canalization
    C. homeostasis
    D. maturation
    E. physiological integration

38. Which of the following authors would you be LEAST likely to recommend for information about child care?

    A. Sidonie Gruenberg
    B. Jean Piaget
    C. Ernest Harms
    D. Benjamin Spock
    E. Arnold Gesell

39. All of the following statements are generally TRUE of children of elementary school age EXCEPT

    A. girls mature approximately one year earlier than do boys
    B. girls have poorer health than boys
    C. girls excel in body balance and fine hand coordination
    D. girls excel in school achievement
    E. girls tend to get their second set of teeth earlier than boys

40. The teacher of a sixth-grade class is likely to find all of the following characteristics among children of this growth level EXCEPT that they

    A. are influenced very little by what their peers do
    B. are beginning to rebel against adult domination
    C. are at a receptive stage for indoctrination of all sorts
    D. enjoy giving assistance to younger children in the lower grades
    E. are beginning to show more discrimination in the selection of possessions and in the care of them

KEY (CORRECT ANSWERS)

1. B	11. C	21. D	31. D
2. C	12. A	22. C	32. C
3. B	13. A	23. E	33. D
4. C	14. B	24. A	34. C
5. A	15. E	25. A	35. E
6. B	16. B	26. D	36. A
7. D	17. C	27. C	37. C
8. A	18. E	28. D	38. B
9. A	19. C	29. D	39. B
10. B	20. D	30. A	40. A

EXAMINATION SECTION
TEST 1

Questions 1-5.

DIRECTIONS: Questions 1 to 5 are based on the following:
For each of the 5 names listed in column I, identify the field of interest in column II with which that name is MOST closely associated. For each of the names listed in column I, write the number of the field of interest identified with it.

I	II
1. Pavlov	A. play therapy
2. Forrester	B. psychoanalytic approach to child therapy
3. Jennings	C. assembly programs
4. Piaget	D. study of conditioning
5. Slavson	E. psychodrama
	F. occupational literature
	G. oral reading tests
	H. study of language development in children
	I. sociometry
	J. mentally gifted

1.____
2.____
3.____
4.____
5.____

Questions 6-10.

DIRECTIONS: Questions 6 to 10 are based on the following:
For each of the 5 names listed in column I, identify the field of interest in column II with which that name is MOST closely associated. For each of the names listed in column I, write the number of the field of interest identified with it.

I	II
6. Levy	A. delinquency
7. Betts	B. adolescence
8. Raths	C. mental diseases
9. Traxler	D. sentence completion tests
10. Hurlock	E. visual difficulty
	F. reading disability
	G. emotional needs
	H. sibling rivalry
	I. exceptional children
	J. survey of study habits

6.____
7.____
8.____
9.____
10.____

Questions 11-50.

DIRECTIONS: Each question or incomplete statement is followed by several suggested answers or completions. Select the one that BEST answers the question or completes the statement. *PRINT THE LETTER OF THE CORRECT ANSWER IN THE SPACE AT THE RIGHT.*

11. Roger, who has a morbid fear of attending school and has been absent all year, is described as suffering from a(n)

    A. psychosis
    B. phobia
    C. inversion
    D. regression

12. The term asexual means

    A. not pertaining to sex
    B. perverted
    C. homosexual
    D. hypersexed

13. The term ambivalent is used to describe a child who

    A. is given to creating dissension among others
    B. makes a statement and later amplifies it with conscious intent
    C. seems to be daydreaming while actually alert
    D. is aggressive at times and friendly at other times

14. A wound or injury to the emotions is called

    A. an illusion
    B. a trauma
    C. hysteria
    D. a delusion

15. A child is psychotic who has a(n)

    A. urge toward some inappropriate sexual behavior
    B. nervous disorder of a functional type
    C. prolonged form of mental derangement
    D. inhibition in his social behavior

16. Of the following terms, the one that applies to the development of wholesome mental and emotional reactions and habits is called

    A. psychoanalysis
    B. psychotherapy
    C. mental hygiene
    D. clinical psychology

17. Studies of children's fantasies show that, in the average elementary school child, fantasies

    A. play an insignificant part in his life
    B. will still be active but are becoming tempered with reality
    C. are an indication of an unsettled inner life
    D. are an indication that the child is unable to face his problems

18. In collecting data for identifying pupil problems, information which compares a child to his peer group is called

    A. ideographic
    B. psychogenic
    C. acculturative
    D. normative

19. If a school child experiences anxiety, which one of the following statements is MOST likely to be true? It may

    A. facilitate learning
    B. catalyze learning
    C. either thwart or facilitate learning
    D. have no effect on learning

20. Of the following, what is the effect of a child's self-concept upon his behavior?

    A. It shifts and/or distorts the perceptions that act as stimuli to behavior.
    B. It functions principally in matters where conformity to or violation of the social code is involved.
    C. Its influence is best described by the Freudian concept of superego.
    D. It enables him to engage in almost superhuman effort.

21. The behavioral scientist's research technique of studying the behavior of the same individual or individuals at succeeding ages is called the

    A. comparative method
    B. continuation method
    C. case method
    D. longitudinal method

22. According to Erikson, the critical developmental task of adolescence is

    A. learning who one is
    B. development of a sense of work and self-discipline
    C. development of adequate peer relations
    D. socialization of his acquisitive instincts

23. Compared to a group of unselected children of the same age, sex, and race, gifted children, on the average,

    A. have a higher incidence of visual defects
    B. reach puberty earlier
    C. are taller, heavier, and stronger
    D. show more personality problems

24. Harry is 17 years old. He is very close to his mother and prefers the company of older women to girls closer to his age. According to psychoanalytic theory, he would MOST likely be regarded as having a(n)

    A. unresolved Oedipus complex
    B. Tantalus complex
    C. homosexual complex
    D. heterosexual complex

25. The MOST frequently occurring mental disorder among youth during the adolescent period is

    A. manic-depressive psychosis
    B. involutional melancholia
    C. schizophrenia
    D. drug hallucinations

26. Fears represent acquired behaviors; thus, fears are subject to systematic modification and elimination. The MOST basic technique for overcoming established fears in school children is

    A. disuse
    B. verbal appeal
    C. reconditioning
    D. sublimation

27. The adolescent is MOST likely to seek the greatest emotional support and understanding from

    A. idealized adults
    B. isolated activity
    C. the peer culture
    D. heterosexual contacts

28. The neonate is to the infant as the pre-adolescent is to the

    A. primary grade child
    B. middle grade child
    C. early adolescent
    D. senescent

29. According to traditional psychoanalytic concepts, the MOST important cause of the neurotic reaction is the "excessive use" of the mechanism of

    A. sublimation
    B. introspection
    C. rationalization
    D. repression

30. The concepts of "field" and "life space," as related to personality theory, are basic derivations of the work of

    A. Sigmund Freud
    B. Leon Festinger
    C. Kurt Lewin
    D. Alfred Adler

31. According to Freudian theory, the person who grows up strongly characterized by orderliness, parsimony, and obstinacy is likely to have experienced disturbance in his

    A. nursing experience
    B. relations with his parent of the opposite sex at about 5 or 6
    C. peer relations during young adulthood
    D. toilet training

32. Which one of the following psychologists would be MOST likely to offer an explanation of the learning process in terms of the reduction of specific needs?

    A. Skinner
    B. Tolman
    C. Adkins
    D. Hull

33. EGO IDENTITY, as used by Leona Tyler, comes closest to the

    A. libido theory of Freud
    B. self-concept theory of Rogers
    C. identification theory of Freud
    D. collective unconscious theory of Jung

34. Freud's instinctual libido theory places emphasis upon

    A. neurosis
    B. condign punishment
    C. anxiety
    D. innate sexuality

35. Stanley, a student whose grades are poor, developed the notion that his grades would improve considerably if he took exams only on even days, such as Tuesdays or Thursdays or on the even hours such as 10, 12, 2, etc. This is an example of

    A. phratry
    B. anxiety neurosis
    C. obsessive-compulsive behavior
    D. hysteria

36. Of the following, which group is principally characterized by perseveration, hyperactivity, and sensitivity to stimuli?

    A. Slow learners
    B. Emotionally disturbed
    C. Brain injured
    D. Severely retarded

37. The classical Lippitt and White study showed that groups were more cohesive in which one of the following "social climates" or atmospheres?

    A. Democratic
    B. Authoritarian
    C. Democratic-autocratic
    D. Laissez-faire

38. Which one of the following is associated with the development of psychodrama as a group experience?

    A. Terman
    B. Spearman
    C. Cattell
    D. Moreno

39. The following description of social change MOST in agreement with Rogers' "self-theory" is that

    A. the group changes as a unit rather than member by member
    B. an equilibrium "set" is necessary after a new level of behavior is reached
    C. a change is most likely to occur when individuals are free to change or not to change
    D. the creation of a state of disequilibrium among the members both precedes and follows change

40. Of the following, the BEST description of the situational leadership theory is

    A. a skilled leader is a successful leader in any situation
    B. the leader's effectiveness differs in relation to the personality differences of the groups
    C. the leader needs less knowledge but more expertise than the members
    D. the leader is the one who has the intelligence and knowledge the situation demands

41. In which of the following personality inventories has an attempt been made to control the factor of social desirability?

    A. California Test of Personality
    B. Edwards Personal Preference Schedule
    C. Bell Adjustment Inventory
    D. Mental Health Analysis

42. Counselors are becoming increasingly concerned about children's self-acceptance and their acceptance of others. At what age is it necessary to begin paying attention to children's feelings about race?

    A. 2 B. 4 C. 8 D. 12

43. Hunt's survey of research on intellectual development concludes that intelligence

    A. is relatively fixed by age 5
    B. is genetically determined
    C. grows out of the child's interaction with environment
    D. is not related to cultural background

44. According to J.P. Guilford's model of intelligence, it is desirable to develop intelligence tests which measure

    A. one general factor of intelligence
    B. one primary and a number of specific factors of intelligence
    C. seven primary factors of intelligence
    D. about 120 distinct factors of intelligence

45. When using a rating scale, it is considered BEST to rate

    A. all persons on one trait before going on to the next trait
    B. one person on all traits before going on to the next person
    C. traits of each person in groups of five
    D. each person on an overall basis before rating traits

46. Successful intra-group relations are MOST impeded by members who

    A. are silent or say very little
    B. try to satisfy personal needs
    C. wander off the subject
    D. do not listen well

47. Which one of the following has MOST to do with change in the performance of group members?

    A. Improvement in ability to think critically
    B. Improvement in the correctness of perceptions
    C. Improvement in the ability to listen
    D. Greater understanding of possible roles

48. If you were planning to organize a counseling group for acting out sixth grade youngsters, which one of the following would be the OPTIMAL size for this purpose?

    A. 2 B. 5 C. 15 D. 20

49. In experiments with varying types of leadership, all of the following were demonstrated EXCEPT

    A. group unity appeared highest in groups with democratic leaders
    B. intra-group aggression was highest in authoritarian groups
    C. attention-seeking behavior was highest in democratic groups
    D. constructiveness of work decreased sharply in authoritarian groups when the leader was absent

50. The most unique aspect of Spearman's theory of intelligence is his assumption that

    A. mental tests are not direct measures of mental ability
    B. intelligence is made up of a large number of specific abilities
    C. intelligence is essentially a unitary trait
    D. intelligence is made up of one general and several specific factors

KEY (CORRECT ANSWERS)

1. D	11. B	21. D	31. D	41. B
2. F	12. A	22. A	32. D	42. B
3. I	13. D	23. C	33. B	43. C
4. H	14. B	24. A	34. D	44. D
5. A	15. C	25. C	35. C	45. A
6. H	16. C	26. C	36. C	46. B
7. E	17. B	27. C	37. A	47. B
8. G	18. D	28. C	38. D	48. B
9. J	19. C	29. D	39. C	49. C
10. B	20. A	30. C	40. B	50. D

TEST 2

DIRECTIONS: Each question or incomplete statement is followed by several suggested answers or completions. Select the one that BEST answers the question or completes the statement. *PRINT THE LETTER OF THE CORRECT ANSWER IN THE SPACE AT THE RIGHT.*

1. In Erickson's theory of ego-identity development, the stage at which the individual must resolve the identity vs. role diffusion crisis is

   A. middle childhood B. adolescence
   C. young adulthood D. middle age

   1.____

2. Learning theorists contend that *undesirable* neurotic symptoms (e.g., phobias) tend to persist because they provide

   A. positive reinforcement or reward
   B. conflict resolution
   C. punishment
   D. negative reinforcement or pain reduction

   2.____

3. According to psychoanalytic theory, psychosexual development progresses through the following stages in which of the sequences below?

   A. Oral, anal, genital, phallic
   B. Anal, oral, genital, phallic
   C. Oral, anal, phallic, genital
   D. Anal, oral, phallic, genital

   3.____

4. A phenomenological position in personality theory implies to a counselor that

   A. the best source of information about a client is the client himself
   B. objective personality tests are more valuable generally than projective techniques
   C. a client is always free to make his own decisions
   D. past learning is of little importance in determining present behavior

   4.____

5. "The failing student fails because he expects himself to fail." This is an example of Lecky's theory of

   A. self-consistency B. self-actualization
   C. internalization D. ego-conflict

   5.____

6. Studies of "ethnocentric" or "prejudiced" children (when compared with "liberal" or "unprejudiced" children) indicate that they have parents who

   A. are little concerned with status
   B. have very close affectionate ties with the child
   C. use harsh and rigid discipline
   D. emphasize social mores rather than conformity

   6.____

7. Piaget would characterize the 11-15 year-old's thought processes as a period of

   A. enactive representation B. concrete thought
   C. sensorimotor activities D. formal operations

   7.____

8. "Creativity" is linked *most closely* with the concept of 8.____

    A. divergent thought   B. productive thought
    C. critical thought   D. reasoning

9. Most theories of motivation appear to be in agreement that human behavior consists *primarily* of 9.____

    A. autogenous responses to external stimuli
    B. imitation of what is expected by others in the culture
    C. inhibition of the drives connected with one's impulses
    D. purposive, goal-directed activity based upon anticipated results of the behavior

10. A group to which an individual relates or aspires to relate himself, such as a political party, a social class, or an occupational group, is called a 10.____

    A. social stratum   B. sub-culture
    C. primary group   D. reference group

11. Kagan and Moss found the GREATEST predictive power of behavior from child to adult to be during ages 11.____

    A. 0-3   B. 2-4   C. 3-6   D. 6-10

12. A modern approach to changing behavior, which is often termed "milieu therapy," would suggest that counselors should spend relatively *more* time in 12.____

    A. giving tests and gathering other psychometric data
    B. working with teachers and parents
    C. having individual therapeutic interviews
    D. engaging in broad public relations activities

13. Jennie, a 15-year-old high school student, had been close to her mother and father, who adored her. Lately, however, Jennie refuses to go with her parents when they visit relatives or simply go out for a ride and dinner. She says she wants to go out with her friends. Jennie's mother is deeply hurt and says, "I don't know what's come over Jennie lately, and we used to be such a tight-knit family."
    From the point of view of adolescent development, Jennie's behavior is *most probably* an example of 13.____

    A. idiopathic withdrawal tendency
    B. exploratory social behavior
    C. rebellion against authority
    D. normal preference for company of peers

14. Guilford's studies of creativity have relied MOST heavily on 14.____

    A. factor analysis
    B. case study
    C. protective test analysis
    D. experimental manipulation

15. Kinsey's studies reveal that, by age 15, the incidence of masturbation among boys is *approximately* 15.____

    A. 52%   B. 67%   C. 82%   D. 97%

16. With respect to general intelligence, delinquent adolescents compared with non-delinquent adolescents are

   A. more intelligent
   B. less intelligent
   C. about equal in intelligence
   D. more or less intelligent, varying with different studies

17. The most common kind of delinquency, sub-cultural or socialized, is characteristic of the lower-class child who turns to a ready-made delinquent culture within his own society. The important thing to remember about this type of delinquency is that it is

   A. not primarily gang delinquency
   B. delinquency in terms of upper-class mores
   C. more likely to be female than male
   D. not delinquency at all

18. Of the following characteristics, the one that should be regarded as MOST indicative of possible maladjustment in a junior high school girl is

   A. interest in art to the virtual neglect of other subjects
   B. striving for perfect marks in all her school work
   C. getting along easily with all her teachers
   D. lack of interest in boys

19. Height and weight curves which have been developed for adolescents show a(n)

   A. *marked spurt* in rate of growth in early adolescence followed by *little change* in later adolescence
   B. *moderately increased rate* in early adolescence followed by a *greatly decreased rate* in later adolescence
   C. *steady rate* of growth throughout the adolescent period
   D. *increased rate* of growth in early adolescence followed by a *gradual slowing down*

20. Studies of the early history of gifted children reveal that, in general, they begin to walk

   A. and to talk at about the same age as typical children
   B. at an earlier age than typical children but begin to talk at about the same age as typical children
   C. at about the same age as typical children but begin to talk at an earlier age than typical children
   D. and to talk at an earlier age than typical children

21. In general, juvenile fiction comprises the major part of the reading choices of

   A. girls between 9 and 13   B. boys of all ages
   C. girls of all ages   D. boys between 12 and 16

22. Of the following, a major recreational activity *common* to both 10 and 15-year-old boys and girls is

   A. going to the movies
   B. riding a bicycle
   C. watching athletic sports
   D. social dancing

23. Girls tend to be superior to boys at the same age in

    A. linguistic fluency
    B. speed of reaction time
    C. arithmetical reasoning
    D. most forms of perception

24. The sequence of developmental stages in MOST children is similar. This phenomenon is known as

    A. acculturation
    B. hypostatization
    C. adaptation
    D. maturation

25. With which of the following authors would the term "extreme endomorphy" be correctly associated?

    A. Sheldon
    B. McLelland
    C. James
    D. Piaget

26. Which of the following is MOST clearly associated with orthodox Freudian psychoanalytic theory?

    A. Stress on the cultural determinants of behavior
    B. Emphasis on infantile development, traumata, sexual needs, and aberrations
    C. Concern with the client's present circumstances and the quality of his interpersonal relationships
    D. Emphasis on counselor-client relationship and the client's perception of that relationship

27. Awareness of and attitudes towards racial differences arise primarily from

    A. parental attitudes
    B. teachings in the church
    C. teachings in the school
    D. prevailing peer attitudes

28. The teachers' interactions with the children in her class would be classified as integrative if she deals with the children in a manner that is

    A. commanding and demanding
    B. flexible, responsive and spontaneous
    C. resistive to suggestions from the children
    D. non-accepting of the independent actions and ideas of the children

29. Among the following, the LEAST valid goal for the group discussion-leader during the *first* sessions with the group is

    A. realization by the group of the distinction between an individual and his unacceptable behavior
    B. encouragement of self-revelation
    C. freedom to express any ideas or feelings for consideration by the group
    D. establishment of goals of mutual helpfulness

30. Among the following, the LEAST valid way for the counselor to encourage a sense of acceptance on the part of everyone in the group is to

    A. be nonjudgmental with respect to all contributions from the group
    B. use the technique of reflection to help clarify statements
    C. give advice when the need is apparent
    D. call attention to existing limits when necessary

31. In basketball teams which have won most of their games, the typical team leader differs from the typical leader of less successful teams *mainly* in

    A. exercising more critical discrimination and seeing more differences among the players on his team
    B. being generally warmer and more reassuring toward all members of his team
    C. being rated higher (by the coach) in his basketball skills than any member of his team
    D. having a higher I.Q.

32. Which principle of developmental direction is illustrated by the fact that infants sit up before learning to walk?

    A. General to specific action
    B. Proximo-distal direction
    C. Motor chaining
    D. Cephalo-caudal direction

33. Studies dealing with stability of I.Q.s of culturally deprived children who stay in underprivileged environments show

    A. a steady decline in median score with age
    B. a stable I.Q. although below the national average
    C. an unpredictable direction of average I.Q. score due to individual differences
    D. slight increase in I.Q. score due to exposure to TV, radio, etc.

34. Studies have shown that children from different social classes learn prejudices at different stages in their development. Compared with the other social classes, the lower-class children generally develop biases

    A. earlier than the other classes
    B. later than the other classes
    C. at about the same stage of development as other classes
    D. unpredictably, depending on the area in which the bias was first encountered

35. Which would NOT be characteristic of mentally retarded children?

    A. Walking and talking is later in infancy than expected for normal children.
    B. A high percentage of speech defects is noted.
    C. Mechanical or motor skills are superior to those of normal children.
    D. Mean height and weight are less than those for normal children.

36. An overprotected child would MOST likely exhibit which of the following group of characteristics in school?

    A. Withdrawal from difficult situations, obedience to the teacher, and self-centeredness
    B. Persistence in difficult situations, obedience to the teacher, and self-centeredness
    C. Domination of the teacher-child relation, self-centeredness, and withdrawal from difficult situations
    D. Domination of the teacher-child relation, self-centeredness, and persistence in difficult situations

37. A compendium, covering many areas of children's social and psychological development and authored by a dozen or more well-known writers in the field, is entitled

    A. WHEN WE KNOW
    B. HELPING SCHOOL CHILDREN TO GROW EMOTIONALLY
    C. HOW TO HELP YOUR CHILDREN
    D. UNDERSTANDING THE CHILD

38. The imaginary companion is a phenomenon of child development which occurs most frequently in ages

    A. 2-3   B. 4-5   C. 6-7   D. 8-9

39. Of the following, the LEAST effective way of dealing with children's fears is

    A. explaining and reassuring
    B. helping the child to face the feared situation
    C. simply ignoring the child's fear
    D. setting examples of fearlessness

40. The age at which individuals cease to grow in intellectual ability is

    A. 13 years   B. 16 years
    C. 21 years   D. probably none of these

41. Surveys of the opinions and attitudes of young people show that adolescent boys and girls find their MOST perplexing problems in the area of

    A. academic activities   B. personal relations
    C. educational choices   D. vocational choices

42. The MOST accurate statement concerning the incidence of physical defects among mentally deficient children, as compared with normal children, is that mentally deficient children have

    A. more physical defects
    B. fewer physical defects
    C. about the same amount of physical defects
    D. more or fewer physical defects, varying in different study populations

43. Among children who have learning difficulties, the greatest incidence of associated organic defects is found in which ONE of the following groups?

   A. Educable mentally retarded
   B. Slow learners
   C. Trainable mentally retarded
   D. Academically retarded

44. Which one of the following statements MOST accurately describes the comparative incidence of speech defects in relation to sex?

   A. Approximately equal percentages of boys and girls have defective speech.
   B. A higher percentage of girls than boys have defective speech.
   C. A higher percentage of boys than girls have defective speech.
   D. There is a lack of agreement about which sex shows more defective speech.

45. According to Kvaraceus, the one of the following which *most likely* represents the delinquent's attitude toward school is

   A. fear and cynicism
   B. hate and hostility
   C. suspicion and doubt
   D. annoyance and amusement

46. When we compare young children and adolescents with respect to the relative effectiveness of distributed and concentrated practice as a learning technique, we find that

   A. young children learn better by distributed practice; adolescents by concentrated practice
   B. young children learn better by concentrated practice; adolescents by distributed practice
   C. both young children and adolescents learn better by concentrated practice
   D. both young children and adolescents learn better by distributed practice

47. A child develops a headache every time a particularly distasteful task is announced. This type of reaction is characterized as

   A. hysterical
   B. rationalization
   C. projection
   D. physiological

48. A teacher organized Section I of his class into five groups of five pupils each. He gave each group problems to solve and recorded their discussions, having first announced that in each group the best member would be marked A; the second best B; the average member C; the remaining two D and F. In Section II, another 25 pupils were also in five groups of five members each. The problems were the same, but in Section II it was announced that all members of the group having the best discussions would get A; all members of the second best group would get B; in the mid-group all would get C; in the next poorer group all members would get D; and in the poorest group everyone would be marked F.
The difference was found to be that

   A. the inter-individual competition resulted in more good ideas produced in Section I than in Section II
   B. members were more friendly to one another in Section II than in Section I
   C. communication difficulties were more noticeable in Section II than in Section I
   D. groups in Section I were more orderly and systematic in their approach to problems

49. Suppose a group of adolescents, previously unacquainted, are brought together in a school or camp. If, from week to week, each indicates his degree of liking for the others and also the extent to which he thinks each of the others shares his own values, the *usual* finding will be that

    A. each intuitively likes best the companions who agree with his values; he chooses them even before he knows their attitude
    B. there is no consistent tendency for similarity of values to be correlated with liking
    C. the tendency is to enjoy difference rather than similarity and to prefer those who challenge rather than confirm one's own values
    D. the correlation between similarity of values and liking is low at first, but increases with longer acquaintance

50. Of the following authors, the one *most closely* associated with a collection of readings designed to serve as a basal text in group counseling and the group process, and in which the various kinds of groups and levels of group functioning are explored is

    A. Margaret E. Bennett B. Walter Lifton
    C. Gratton Kemp D. S.R. Slavson

KEY (CORRECT ANSWERS)

1. B	11. D	21. A	31. A	41. B
2. D	12. B	22. A	32. D	42. A
3. C	13. D	23. A	33. A	43. C
4. A	14. A	24. D	34. A	44. C
5. A	15. C	25. A	35. C	45. B
6. C	16. B	26. B	36. A	46. D
7. D	17. D	27. A	37. C	47. A
8. A	18. B	28. B	38. B	48. B
9. D	19. D	29. B	39. C	49. D
10. D	20. D	30. C	40. D	50. C

EXAMINATION SECTION
TEST 1

DIRECTIONS: Each question or incomplete statement is followed by several suggested answers or completions. Select the one that BEST answers the question or completes the statement. *PRINT THE LETTER OF THE CORRECT ANSWER IN THE SPACE AT THE RIGHT.*

1. In general, which of the following would be of more concern to a psychotherapist than to a counselor? Problems of

    A. vocational-educational planning
    B. a person's appropriate "role"
    C. intrapersonal conflict
    D. interpersonal conflict

    1.____

2. The Davis and Havighurst studies on the effects of socio-economic class on children show that the lower-class child

    A. has less intellectual potential and, therefore, does not profit from school as much as the middle-class child
    B. has about the same expectations about school as does the middle-class child
    C. has untapped potential of intellectual ability because the school does not understand his ways
    D. should not be handicapped by his background and so should do well in school

    2.____

3. When a dog learns to withdraw his foot from a grid at the sound of a bell and, in doing so, avoids the electric shock, the bell is considered the

    A. unconditioned stimulus
    B. conditioned stimulus
    C. unconditioned response
    D. conditioned response

    3.____

4. Psychoanalytic theory postulates that each child moves through three stages of growth in the following sequential order:

    A. Oral, anal, and genital
    B. Anal, oral, and genital
    C. Genital, anal, and oral
    D. Oral, genital, and anal

    4.____

5. According to psychoanalytic theory, the primary construct for maintaining psychological adjustment between various psychological forces and the external environment is the

    A. libido
    B. id
    C. superego
    D. ego

    5.____

6. The method whereby an investigator is able to study, within a relatively short period of time, the typical behavior of children at different stages of development is called the

    A. cross-sectional approach
    B. longitudinal approach
    C. experimental approach
    D. analytical approach

    6.____

7. Data about a child's behavior and development derived from official records, parental and teacher interviews, as well as the child's own account, is referred to as the

   A. autobiographical method
   B. case-history method
   C. psychoanalytic method
   D. self-system method

8. A quick means for determining the reading group in which an eight-year-old should be placed would be through the use of the

   A. Gray Oral Reading Paragraphs
   B. Gates Survey I
   C. Monroe Silent Reading Test
   D. New York Tests of Growth in Reading

9. The theorists who hold that learning to read involves seeing wholes first, learning details later, and then learning without awareness of details, are referred to as

   A. gestaltists
   B. behaviorists
   C. existentialists
   D. neo-Freudianists

10. The BEST way for an adult to help a child cope with fear is to

    A. consistently ignore the fear
    B. ridicule
    C. force him into the feared situation
    D. provide for positive reconditioning through success and pleasantness

11. Of the following, the MOST distinguishing characteristic of middle childhood is

    A. identification with figures outside his family
    B. interest in persons of the opposite sex
    C. attempting to act like adults
    D. need for and dependence on adults

12. The hormone MOST active in intense emotional reactions has been found to be

    A. cortisone
    B. adrenaline
    C. thyroxin
    D. dexedrine

13. An individual, when in the presence of a figure reminiscent of a feared father, feels himself getting sweaty, tense, and frightened ("Anxious"). This style of reactivity BEST illustrates

    A. reaction formation
    B. stimulus generalization
    C. response generalization
    D. approach-avoidance behavior

14. The aspect of intellectual functioning MOST likely to be negatively affected by the testing of a depressed individual is his

    A. abstract thinking
    B. social judgment
    C. speed of mental processes
    D. word understanding (vocabulary)

15. The concept of the "self-actualization needs" of the individual is MOST frequently associated with the name of

   A. Leon Festinger
   B. Abraham H. Maslow
   C. Alfred C. Kinsey
   D. O. Hobart Mowrer

16. Of the following, the MOST frequent cause of neurotic behavior in school-age children is

   A. inadequate teachers; maladjusted, authoritarian, rigid personalities
   B. inappropriate curriculum for their level of ability
   C. unhealthy parent-child relationships and poor identification model in the home
   D. cultural and social deprivation

17. In order to understand how some home situation is affecting a child's development, it is MOST helpful, of the following, to know

   A. some basic psychoanalytic principles
   B. the past experience of the parents
   C. how the situation came about
   D. how the child views the situation

18. Groups, characterized by more or less intimate face-to-face association and cooperation, are primary groups. Which one of the following is NOT a primary group?

   A. The family
   B. The gang
   C. Adolescent play groups
   D. Special interest groups

19. The groups to which an individual belongs and feels a loyalty are called in-groups; those toward which he feels neither loyalty nor sympathy are called out-groups. The in-group versus out-group pattern results from

   A. basic human nature
   B. clash of social norms
   C. individual differences
   D. cooperative competition

20. The leader of a group of 12-year-old girls is MOST likely to be superior to the other members of the group in

   A. ability to make friends
   B. appearance
   C. school work
   D. artistic or musical talent

21. Of the following, the single characteristic MOST important in determining an individual's status in a group of pre-adolescent boys is

   A. intelligence
   B. physical ability
   C. school marks
   D. language development

22. Studies of small groups of individuals have indicated that the greatest amount of aggressive behavior is noted in situations in which the control manifested by an adult leader may be characterized as

   A. autocratic
   B. democratic
   C. laissez-faire
   D. permissive

23. Of the following, the MOST important condition underlying the formation of an out-of-school group of eleven-year-old girls is

   A. coming from the same socio-economic level
   B. showing the same signs of physical development
   C. having the same attitudes and interests
   D. being in the same grade at school

24. Recent studies of the productivity of individuals while working as members of a group on a joint project having demonstrated that

   A. larger groups are more productive than smaller groups working on similar tasks
   B. individuals function in much the same way in groups as they do in solitary situations
   C. a group goal is needed to motivate individuals to higher levels of performance
   D. high school pupils work better in groups; college students, as individuals

25. The acceptance of an individual by an already functioning group will depend MOST upon the

   A. extent to which the individual accepts the group's norms of behavior
   B. contribution the individual can make to realization of the group's goals
   C. influence which the individual enjoys in the community as a whole
   D. ability of the individual to provoke the group to concerted action

26. Of the following, the MOST important single factor contributing to the success of a program of therapy with a seriously maladjusted child is the

   A. length of time which can be given to therapeutic work
   B. relationship which is established between the child and the therapist
   C. mental level of the child
   D. extent of adherence to a particular theoretical orientation on the part of the therapist

27. Studies of the early history of gifted children reveal that, in general, they begin to walk

   A. and to talk at about the same age as typical children
   B. at an earlier age than typical children but begin to talk at about the same age as typical children
   C. at about the same age as typical children but begin to talk at an earlier age than typical children
   D. and to talk at an earlier age than typical children

28. Height and weight curves which have been developed for adolescents show

   A. a marked spurt in rate of growth in early adolescence followed by little change in later adolescence
   B. a moderately increased rate in early adolescence followed by a greatly increased rate in later adolescence
   C. a steady rate of growth throughout the adolescent period
   D. an increased rate of growth in early adolescence followed by a gradual slowing down

29. As compared to girls, boys begin their adolescent development

   A. later, and reach maturity later
   B. later, and reach maturity sooner
   C. earlier, and reach maturity sooner
   D. earlier, and reach maturity later

30. The 15-year-old boy whose physiological development has been slower than that of his peers tends to

   A. compensate by showing unusual interest in girls
   B. become fatigued and fall behind in group activities
   C. develop unwholesome personality characteristics, such as aggression
   D. exhibit lack of interest in the typical activities in which his peers engage

31. Of the following characteristics, the one that should be regarded as MOST indicative of possible maladjustment in an 8th-grade girl is

   A. interest in art to the virtual neglect of other subjects
   B. striving for perfect marks in all her school work
   C. getting along easily with all her teachers
   D. lack of interest in boys

32. Of the following characteristics, the one MOST generally found among children just entering the junior high school is

   A. a tendency of boys and girls to seek each other's company
   B. the acceptance of parent and teacher opinion with little question
   C. the popularity of guessing games, puzzles, and games of chance
   D. a preference for highly organized competitive team play

33. Which of the following groups of behaviors is considered MOST serious by psychologists?

   A. Heterosexual activity, masturbation, writing obscene notes
   B. Depression, fearfulness, unsocialness
   C. Cruelty, domineering, resentfulness
   D. Overcriticalness, sensitiveness, dreaminess

34. Sheldon and Eleanor Glueck, in their analysis of the family situations of 1,000 juvenile delinquents, discovered that among the following, the factor of highest frequency was that

   A. one or both parents had had no schooling
   B. families had at one time been known to family welfare agencies
   C. mothers worked to supplement family income
   D. parents were either separated or divorced

35. The endocrine gland which has the greatest influence in regulating physical growth throughout life is the

   A. pituitary   B. thyroid
   C. thymus   D. pineal

36. Of the following, the author who is credited as the one who began the scientific study of delinquency is

    A. William Healy
    B. Frederick Thrasher
    C. Clifford Shaw
    D. William Kvaraceus

37. Adolescence is a developmental period of renewed stresses on the individual. In the following factors, the one to which the adolescent is LEAST responsive is to

    A. be psychologically identified with peer groups
    B. gain acceptance and approval of behavior from adults
    C. conform to the customs and practices of adolescent groups
    D. gain a sense of goal direction or major purpose

38. There is general acceptance of certain basic concepts by different school of psychoanalytic thought. However, one concept which is not universally accepted among such schools is that

    A. human behavior is deterministic
    B. a dynamic unconscious influences behavior
    C. a neurosis is the result of unresolved oedipal conflict
    D. a genetic approach is necessary to the understanding of behavior

39. Of the following statements, the one that is conceptually a correct representation of topological psychology, originated by Kurt Lewin, is that it

    A. applies, for the first time, principles of field theory to events of behavior and consciousness
    B. applies concepts of mathematics and physics in explaining the structure of behavior
    C. holds that motivation seldom has a place in explaining human behavior
    D. supports the theory that drill without understanding is more effective in learning than a problem-solving approach

40. The endocrine gland which is called the "master gland" because its several hormones play a crucial role in the growth and development of the body and in the regulation of other glands and body processes is the

    A. thyroid
    B. pituitary
    C. parathyroid
    D. adrenal

41. Of the following responses to emotional frustration, the one which is generally considered socially acceptable is

    A. rationalization
    B. projection
    C. regression
    D. sublimation

42. Boys and girls are generally MOST inclined toward group experiences with members of their own sex when they are between

    A. 4 and 5 years of age
    B. 6 and 10 years of age
    C. 11 and 14 years of age
    D. 15 and 18 years of age

43. Of the following, the MOST acceptable definition of the term "exceptional children" is that they are children who

    A. are either intellectually gifted or mentally defective, the physically handicapped and the emotionally disturbed
    B. display unusual talent in the fields of art and music
    C. should be accelerated in school through rapid advancement
    D. should be referred for clinical help

44. A psychological theory which has influenced the teaching field through its contributions to the understanding of human behavior in terms of adjustment is the

    A. reinforcement theory
    B. Gestalt theory
    C. topological theory
    D. psychoanalytic theory

45. The scientific method was introduced formally into psychology when

    A. John Dewey initiated the functional approach to psychology
    B. Sigmund Freud spoke out strongly and persuasively for consideration of unconscious influences
    C. Wilhelm Wundt opened his Psychological Institute at the University of Leipzig
    D. John B. Watson introduced behaviorism into American psychology

46. The term "superego" as used in psychoanalytic discussions may BEST be defined as

    A. moral conscience
    B. improper impulses
    C. feelings of inferiority
    D. the id forces

47. The two functional units of the autonomic nervous system are the

    A. endocrine and central systems
    B. endocrine and sympathetic systems
    C. central and parasympathetic systems
    D. sympathetic and parasympathetic systems

48. The defense mechanism by which a person attributes a wish or impulse of his own to another person is known as

    A. displacement
    B. projection
    C. identification
    D. association

49. The Gestalt theory of learning emphasizes

    A. the integration of the components of a learning situation
    B. learning as a behavioristic process of conditioning of response
    C. stimuli or situations and the responses to these situations
    D. the disciplinary effects of difficult content, rote memory and drill

50. The word association test, modifications of which are in use today in psychological diagnosis, was originated by

    A. Jung
    B. Freud
    C. Thorndike
    D. Binet

KEY (CORRECT ANSWERS)

1. C	11. A	21. B	31. B	41. D
2. C	12. B	22. A	32. C	42. B
3. B	13. B	23. D	33. B	43. A
4. A	14. C	24. C	34. B	44. D
5. D	15. B	25. A	35. A	45. C
6. A	16. C	26. B	36. A	46. A
7. B	17. D	27. D	37. B	47. D
8. A	18. D	28. D	38. C	48. B
9. A	19. B	29. A	39. B	49. A
10. D	20. A	30. D	40. B	50. A

TEST 2

DIRECTIONS: Each question or incomplete statement is followed by several suggested answers or completions. Select the one that BEST answers the question or completes the Statement. *PRINT THE LETTER OF THE CORRECT ANSWER IN THE SPACE AT THE RIGHT.*

1. Changes in cognitive behavior between childhood and adolescence are in the direction of greater

    A. comprehension of abstractions
    B. reliance on concrete realities
    C. dependence on direct experience
    D. emphasis on intuitive functioning

    1._____

2. Gesell refers to the child's development between the ages of six and ten as

    A. an ever-widening spiral
    B. a task phase
    C. a latency period
    D. the transition period

    2._____

3. A defense mechanism defined as the adoption of an attitude opposite to one that proceeds anxiety is

    A. regression
    B. reaction formation
    C. fantasy
    D. identification

    3._____

4. Experiments with the reactions of varying age groups to snakes indicated that, in general, the greatest fear was exhibited by

    A. infants
    B. pre-schoolers
    C. latency age children
    D. adults

    4._____

5. As children get older, the differences in ability between the bright and the dull tend to

    A. become smaller
    B. become greater
    C. stay about the same
    D. vary unpredictably

    5._____

6. Which one of the following descriptions is characteristic of the actively-rejectant home?

    A. Parents show highly emotional attitude, warmth without understanding.
    B. Parents tend to use severe punishment only if bothered.
    C. Parents restrict child's independence with many rules and required obedience.
    D. Child is expected to make his own decisions, although advice is available.

    6._____

7. Homesickness is an example of which type of adjustment mechanism?

    A. Compensation
    B. Identification
    C. Reaction formation
    D. Regression

    7._____

8. Children below the age of 10 when asked to write on "The person I would like to be" most frequently want to emulate

    A. peers
    B. older siblings
    C. parents
    D. real or imaginary glamorous adults

    8._____

9. When a child strikes out at a person who did not provoke the anger, the child is manifesting

   A. repression
   B. regression
   C. over compensation
   D. displaced aggression

10. Of the following, the consonant sound which the average young child is able to articulate before the others is

    A. r   B. b   C. l   D. f

11. Research in the field of language growth of young children indicates that

    A. "only children" tend to surpass in language development children who have siblings
    B. twins generally tend to progress more rapidly in language development than do children of single birth
    C. boys are generally more shy than girls and ask fewer questions
    D. the child who associates more frequently with adults than with other children develops less rapidly in language

12. All of the following statements about habit formation in early childhood are true EXCEPT

    A. guidance in habit formation is unnecessary
    B. many important habits are the basis for habits formed later on
    C. childhood habits are the basis for habits formed later on
    D. the child should build adequate and correct habits by trying to do all things as well as he can

13. The rate and pattern of early motor development of children depend MAINLY upon

    A. maturation
    B. training
    C. experience
    D. acculturation

14. Evidence is accumulating to the effect that the pre-school years are

    A. a period during which all pupils learn at the same rate
    B. a period when very little intellectual growth takes place
    C. not unlike any other age level with respect to intellectual growth
    D. an optimum period for rapid intellectual growth

15. Of an incoming first grader, a teacher may reasonably expect to find that

    A. he expresses his thoughts in complete simple sentences
    B. his dialogue consists of several ideas which are connected by "and" or "and then"
    C. he develops concepts inductively through comparatives such as "taller" and superlatives such as "earliest"
    D. he conveys information through the use of casual connections such as "because" or "in order that"

16. In classical conditioning, extinction occurs when

    A. the conditioned stimulus is presented but not the unconditioned stimulus
    B. the unconditioned stimulus is presented but not the conditioned stimulus
    C. neither the conditioned nor the unconditioned stimuli are presented
    D. both the conditioned and unconditioned stimuli are presented

17. Thorndike is to "reward" as

    A. Hull is to "reinforcement"
    B. Lewin is to "orgone"
    C. Rogers is to "perception"
    D. Skinner is to "contiguity"

18. One would expect the concept of "expectancy" to be emphasized by learning theorists who accept the point of view advanced by

    A. Lewin   B. Skinner
    C. Hull   D. Tolman

19. Of the following, which statement concerning Thorndike's laws of learning would be considered most acceptable by contemporary psychologists? Thorndike's laws

    A. are applicable only to the learning of skills
    B. are applicable to the learning of the lower animals, but not to that of humans
    C. provide a description of the neuromuscular changes occurring during learning
    D. provide a description of factors that promote or hinder learning

20. With regard to the reinforcing effect of changes in level of stimulation, recent findings indicate that

    A. only a decrease in stimulation is reinforcing
    B. only an increase in stimulation is reinforcing
    C. neither an increase or a decrease in stimulation is reinforcing
    D. either an increase or a decrease may be reinforcing

21. In expounding his views on existential psychology, Allport directly criticized learning models in psychological theory because he felt they were

    A. incorrect
    B. too limited in scope
    C. irrelevant to contemporary life
    D. meaningful only in regard to animal behavior

22. Habitual responses that have been acquired under conditions of aperiodic reinforcement tend to

    A. fluctuate erratically   B. extinguish slowly
    C. extinguish quickly   D. generalize widely

23. With repeated practice on a series of similar problems, it is frequently found that organisms require fewer and fewer trials to learn. This is an example of

    A. cue integration   B. learning set
    C. response facilitation   D. error suppression

24. Attempts to provide systematic training to improve generalized aptitude for creative thinking and performance

    A. suggest that very little can be gained through such training
    B. have floundered because of inadequate techniques for training
    C. show great promise for the future
    D. are inconclusive because of lack of control groups

25. Regarding the role of reward in learning, a controversy in the psychological literature still exists between

   A. reinforcement theorists and contiguity theorists
   B. operant theorists and behavior theorists
   C. cognitive theorists and field theorists
   D. psychoanalytic theorists and psycholinguistic theorists

26. Jerome Bruner's description of the changing concept of transfer of training in learning emphasizes

   A. mastery of facts and techniques
   B. teaching and learning materials
   C. teaching and learning of structure
   D. mastery of the humanities

27. Which of the following is the most important step in preparing an animal for learning experiments?

   A. Acculturation to the apparatus
   B. Deprivation of food
   C. Exposure to negative stimuli
   D. Development of confidence in the experimenter

28. Studies of anxiety and its effect on learning generally support the following conclusion about high-anxiety subjects. They do

   A. equally well on simple and complex tasks
   B. well or poorly, unpredictably, on simple and complex tasks
   C. poorly on simple tasks, but do well on complex tasks
   D. well on simple tasks, but do poorly on complex tasks

29. At the present time, the most comprehensive analysis of educational goals is to be found in

   A. the summary report of the Eight Year Study of Progressive Education
   B. the publications of the Educational Policies Commission
   C. John Dewey's HUMAN NATURE AND CONDUCT and EXPERIENCE AND EDUCATION
   D. the TAXONOMY OF EDUCATIONAL OBJECTIVES

30. A learning program based on classical behaviorism would stress

   A. conditioning   B. thinking
   C. understanding   D. volitional activity

31. When stimuli are perceived as emotional, they will

   A. dominate the learning process
   B. influence the learning process
   C. disrupt the learning process
   D. control the learning process

32. The *most important* influence in the learning of social attitudes is the   32._____

    A. family   B. community
    C. church   D. television

33. A truant is *most often* a(n)   33._____

    A. aggressive child
    B. passive child
    C. well-adjusted child who dislikes school
    D. frustrated child

34. Piaget characterized children as MOST egocentric during the period of their   34._____

    A. adolescence   B. puberty
    C. early childhood   D. infancy

35. That the use of corporal punishment by a parent on a child is deplored by the proponents   35._____
    of ego psychology is BEST explained by the fact that the practice

    A. fosters inner motivation in the child to control undesirable impulses
    B. promotes guilt feelings in a parent, but not in a child
    C. inhibits the development of a reliable conscience in the child
    D. violates the tenet of ego psychologists that punishment is unacceptable in child rearing

36. Anxiety found in a child having a school phobia *invariably* originates in the child's fear of   36._____

    A. being enclosed
    B. being separated from his mother
    C. having to prove himself
    D. teachers

37. Of the following, the CORRECT statement is: 37._____

    A. Emotional maturity comes with physical maturity.
    B. The emotionally mature person feels the need to "prove" himself.
    C. Self understanding is not essential to achieving emotional maturity.
    D. Emotional maturity enables one to adjust to environmental changes.

38. Articulate speech should begin when the child is   38._____

    A. around ten months of age
    B. between eighteen months and two years old
    C. in his third year
    D. under fifteen months of age

39. Schizophrenia in children usually becomes manifest   39._____

    A. during the latency period
    B. during adolescence only
    C. when the mother has a history of schizophrenia
    D. during early childhood or adolescence

40. Dementia praecox is now commonly called

   A. schizophrenic reaction
   B. depressive reaction
   C. manic reaction
   D. obsessive reaction

41. The psychologist's report on a child states that he suffers from aphasia. Aphasia is a(n)

   A. impairment of the ability to use or understand spoken language
   B. disturbance of muscular coordination
   C. neurotic reaction characterized by intense fear
   D. inability consciously to recall events or personal identity

42. Many family research experts believe that the relationship between parent and child in this country has a great influence on the personality and development of the child. Which of the following statements BEST represents the opinion of most of these experts concerning parental influence in the child's personality development?

   A. Mothers and fathers have approximately equal impact on their children, regardless of the age or sex of the child.
   B. Fathers have very little impact on their children until the child is 16, after which they have approximately equal impact with the mother.
   C. Mothers and fathers tend to have different effects on their children, depending partly on the age and sex of both parent and child.
   D. The mother's influence on the child, regardless of the sex of the child, is overwhelming up to the age of six, after which the father's influence is predominant, regardless of the sex of the child.

43. A growing child needs group activity in order to develop socially. A gang is one example of such a group. Joining a gang often answers a boy's needs for companionship and adventure. He gets the feeling of belonging and of loyalty to the group. If the gang is delinquent, the tougher the boy is, the more recognition he gets from the gang. He may also find the discipline he needs because gangs frequently develop their own codes and rules of behavior and demand that their members rigidly abide by them.
   On the basis of the foregoing statement, if a child joins a gang, which of the following is *most probably* TRUE?

   A. He will become an adult criminal.
   B. He could not find enough companionship and sense of belonging outside the gang.
   C. The gang was formed to commit acts of violence.
   D. He has been in a detention facility several times already.

44. There are many theories of the causes of delinquent behavior. One approach sees delinquent behavior as the normal response of many adolescents to conditions of social and economic deprivation characteristic of the lower class. This statement *implies* that

   A. delinquent behavior is a neurotic response to repeated personal failure
   B. the root of the delinquency problem is to be found in destructive family relationships
   C. delinquency is more related to a particular kind of social environment than it is to individual character
   D. delinquent behavior can be treated by modifying individual patterns of personal feeling, behavior, and relationships

45. Catastrophic reaction is a characteristic generally attributed to

   A. mental retardates
   B. profoundly deaf children
   C. geniuses
   D. brain-injured persons

46. A children's counselor under your supervision complains that a child in her group misbehaves often by quarreling with the other children, more often when the counselor is present. As a senior children's counselor, you should advise her that this child

   A. obviously needs psychiatric help
   B. is probably expressing her need for attention
   C. should be punished for this behavior
   D. should be transferred to another group

47. Most children do not want to go to bed. Of the following, the BEST technique for a children's counselor to use in getting the children in his group to go to bed is to

   A. provide very strenuous recreational activities before bedtime so that the children will become tired quickly
   B. let them know that bedtime is approaching so they can finish what they are doing
   C. warn them that they will be punished if they do not go to bed on time
   D. tell them that the hour for bedtime was set for their own good

48. The imaginative transposing of oneself into the thinking, feeling, and acting of another, and so structuring the world "as he does" BEST describes the concept of

   A. empathy
   B. rapport
   C. conditioning
   D. exclusion

49. I know what my parents expect of me; I know what teachers demand. I know what the other fellows in my crowd want me to do. I have a dim idea of what my girl wants from me. But I don't know what I want for myself. This statement illustrates the central adolescent problem of

   A. identity
   B. peer group conformity
   C. youth culture
   D. socialization

50. Dr. Nathan Ackerman, a psychiatrist, suggests that "the stability of the family and of its members hinges on a delicate pattern of emotional balance and interchange." Which of the following statements is NOT consistent with this point of view?

   A. The behavior of each family member is affected by every other.
   B. A shift in the emotional interaction of one pair of persons in a given family rarely alters the interaction processes of other family pairs.
   C. In a triangular relationship, one member may bind or disrupt the psychic unity of the other two.
   D. The emotional illness of one family member may complement that of another or may have effects that are antagonistic.

KEY (CORRECT ANSWERS)

1. A	11. A	21. B	31. B	41. A
2. A	12. A	22. B	32. A	42. C
3. B	13. A	23. B	33. D	43. B
4. D	14. D	24. C	34. A	44. C
5. B	15. A	25. A	35. A	45. D
6. C	16. A	26. C	36. B	46. B
7. D	17. A	27. B	37. D	47. B
8. C	18. D	28. D	38. B	48. A
9. D	19. D	29. D	39. D	49. A
10. B	20. D	30. A	40. A	50. B

CHILD DEVELOPMENT

I - MIDDLE YEARS: AGES 6-12

The ages six to twelve are commonly known as the middle years of childhood. This is the time when children are in full bloom: they are no longer babies but the demands of adult life are still far away. All through this period children continue to develop their special personalities. They are getting to know more about themselves and the world in which they live, and their slow, steady growth can be observed. They grow in independence and are more able to take care of themselves. They also are eager adventurers who learn from their explorations but who often find, to their dismay and to the dismay of the adults around them, that they still have a lot to learn.

Each child is different and there are no set rules for rearing or teaching children. How children grow depends on the characteristics they inherit from their parents and, to a great extent, it depends on the guidance provided by parents and other adults. It also depends on the experiences they have inside and outside of their homes.

Although each child's temperament makes her special, certain guidelines of child growth apply to most youngsters, and parents and other caregivers may find these guidelines helpful when working with the middle-years child.

Physical Development

Growth is of many different kinds and a child's development during the middle years includes increases in height, weight, and strength. The different rates of growth of various body parts account for the awkwardness of the youngster in the late childhood years. Height and weight increase much more slowly and evenly during the middle years than in early childhood. Children usually gain about two or three inches in height each year. Just as height increases at a slow steady pace, so, too, does weight. At the age of six, a child will be about seven times his birth weight. For example, a child who weighed seven pounds at birth will weigh almost fifty pounds at age six. Body proportions also change. The trunk becomes slimmer and more elongated in contrast to the chunky body of the preschooler. The chest becomes broader and flatter, causing the shoulders to droop. Arms and legs become long and thin with little evidence of muscles. It is this thinning-out of the trunk, combined with the elongation of the arms and legs, that gives the middle-years child the "all arms and legs" gawky appearance.

Sexual Differentiation

During the middle years, boys and girls gradually become aware of sexual differences in behavior, attitudes, and manners. These sex differences still can be seen in many play activities. Fortunately, however, both boys and girls now receive more encouragement to try activities traditionally reserved for the opposite sex. This helps to break down sex-role stereotypes. For example, girls learn that they can be good at tasks requiring physical skill, and boys learn that they can be caring young persons without losing their "masculinity." Opportunities for different kinds of play also mean that children develop a variety of skills to carry with them into adulthood.

Psychological Development

Middle-years children can find themselves in conflict with the need to grow up and the desire to remain a child forever, a conflict known as the Peter Pan fantasy. They want to grow up so that they can enjoy the prerogatives of adult life: staying up late, driving the car, wearing adult-styled clothes, and being privy to adult secrets. They want to be able to understand and laugh at adult jokes and be accepted into adult confidences and discussions.

On the other hand, they also want to hold on to all the privileges of childhood. Boys who quarrel, fight, and roughhouse and girls who dress up in their mothers' clothing and makeup are regarded as amusing by adults who would not tolerate such behavior in teenagers.

Social Development

There is a culture of childhood that is passed on solely by oral tradition. Many childrens' games, like hopscotch, marbles, kick-the-can, and blindman's buff, are passed down verbally from one generation to the next. Jokes, riddles, and sayings also are transmitted orally.

Georgie Porgie, pudding and pie Kissed the girls and made them cry.
or
Sticks and stones may break my bones, But names will never hurt me.
or
Ladybug, ladybug fly away home. Your house is on fire your children are gone Except for the little one under the stone Ladybug, ladybug fly away home.
or
Rain, rain go away
Come again another day.

This culture of childhood that finds itself rooted in the past gives a clue to the child's relationship to her family. In contrast to the upheaval an adolescent experiences, the young child may appear to be a staid traditionalist who accepts the authority of the family just as she accepts the games and superstitions of previous generations of children. The middle-years child is more likely to defend than attack her family and what it stands for. The family is the main base of security and identity and is still more important than the child's peer group.

Ages and Stages

Information presented here about the ages and stages of children is only a *guide* for adults working with children. Physically, emotionally, and intellectually, each child grows and develops at his own rate. Some youngsters may be early bloomers. That is, they may have reached a stage of emotional or physical development beyond their chronological years. It is not unusual for a six-year-old to be as tall as a ten-year-old. But when interacting with this child, adults must remember that he *is* six and not ten and they should not expect him to behave as though he were a ten-year-old. Another example is an eight-year-old with an extensive vocabulary who can converse with adults as though she were twelve. In a relationship with this child, it is important for adults to remember that although she may be conversationally mature, she may be mentally, physically and emotionally still an eight-year-old.

Understanding the characteristics of an age can be helpful to adults who work with or care for children. But, if adults are to foster optimal growth and development in children, they also must remain sensitive and responsive to children as individuals.

Six-Year-Olds

General
The sixth year is the age of transition.
• At this age, children are active, outgoing, and self-centered. Their own activities take precedence over everything else.
• They are in constant motion: jiggling, shoving, and pushing. They like to roughhouse and their play may go too far because they don't know when to stop.
• They can play organized games with rules, but only at beginning levels because strategy and foresight are not highly developed at the age of six.
• Six-year-olds may be clumsy and tend to dawdle. For example, they may be slow at dressing to go to school or other places. On the other hand, they want their needs met at once and get upset when adults do not drop everything to do their bidding.

Self-Concept and Independence
• They want to be the center of everything to be first and to win. They are the center of their very own universe and their way of

doing things seems the best and only way. They do not lose gracefully or accept criticism.

• They are assertive, bossy, and extremely sensitive to real or imagined slights. They dominate every situation and are always ready with advice.

• Growing up may be a strain at times for six-year-olds and there may be a period of regression during which they engage in baby talk and display babyish behavior.

• Six-year-olds are extremely possessive of their belongings.

• When the outside world impinges adversely upon them, they are stubborn, obstinate, and unreasonable.

• They tend to project their own feelings onto others and then criticize other people because of this. "She thinks she's-everything" or "He's so fresh."

• They are ashamed of their mistakes and fears and of being seen crying and are careful not to expose themselves to criticism.

Relating to Other Children and Adults

• Six-year-olds often pair up and have best friends with whom they spend a good deal of time. Such pairs often take pleasure in "keeping out" a third child who wants to join them.

• Friendships are erratic and may change many times. Lots of tattling and putting-down of other children goes on, for example, "He's dumb."

• Boys and girls occasionally play together at this age, but the movement toward same-sexed friends has already begun.

• Six-year-olds can be highly sensitive to their parents' moods. For instance, they are quick to notice changes in facial expressions.

Although the six-year-old is most loving of his mother, he is also building his sense of self by trying to break away from her. Many temper tantrums are directed at her and the six-year-old may often refuse to obey his mother's directions. On the other hand, the six-year-old can be sympathetic toward his mother when she is not feeling well.

Parents can find the six-year-old trying. Adults working with six-year-olds need to keep a sense of perspective and their sense of humor. If parents and other caregivers remember the transitional nature of this age, six will become a more manageable and less trying age.

Games and Activities

• Their activities center on the physical. Riding a bicycle is an activity they enjoy. Roller skating and swimming also are favorites.

• They are poor at games requiring strategy and foresight like chess, checkers, and tic-tac-toe, but like running games such as tag and hide-and-seek.

• Six-year-olds like making things as well as cooking activities. They also like to paint, color, and draw.

Seven-Year-Olds

General

Seven is the age of quieting down.

• Toward the beginning of the seventh year the child begins to assimilate the wealth of new experiences and information she learned in first grade.

• They begin to sift and sort information into categories and link the bits of information that they have acquired. Seven-year-olds begin to reason and may at times appear serious and reflective.

• Seven-year-olds can be moody and brooding and pensive and sad because their assimilation of knowledge is not always smooth. Action has shifted and may now take place within their minds rather than within a physical space.

• Although they are self-absorbed they are not isolationists. They are becoming more aware not only of themselves, but of others as well.

Self-Concept and Independence

• The increased introspection of seven-year-olds also means that they have an increased sense of self and are acquiring sensitivity to the reactions of others. This sensitivity is to what others do and say, but not to what other people think. To the seven-year-old, thinking and doing are the same thing.

• They are sensitive about their bodies, which they do not like to have exposed or touched, and they may refuse to use the bathroom at school if it has no door on it.

• Because the physical self and the psychic self are so closely related at this stage, seven-year-olds are reluctant to expose themselves to failure and criticism. They often leave the scene rather than put themselves in a position where they might be subject to criticism or disapproval.

Relating to Other Children and Adults

• They want to be helpful and to become real members of the family group.

• They can take on tasks and responsibilities. When performing chores, they are careful and persistent, and they will demand guidance from adults as to "What do we do now?" or "How do we do this?"

• They can be polite and considerate toward adults. Seven-year-olds are less resistant and less stubborn than six-year-olds.

• They play easily with other children and seem to be in control. Although they are active and boisterous, they know when to stop before someone gets hurt.

Games and Activities

• Seven-year-olds have more capacity to play alone than they had at six, and they enjoy solitary activities such as reading and drawing.

• Group play is still not well organized and is carried out to individual ends.

• They like building things but need to know where things go and where they end. They can understand a simple model and a blueprint.

• Seven-year-olds continue to skate, swim, and are better at bike riding.

• They are avid collectors of anything and everything from stones to bottle tops.

• Seven-year-olds are fond of table games and jigsaw puzzles and can tackle a complicated game like Monopoly.

Eight-Year-Olds
General

Eight-year-olds are expansive, but on a higher level than when they were six.

• They are outgoing, curious, and extremely social and self-confident.

• They tend to be critical of themselves and judgmental of others.

• They now concern themselves with the why of events, and they are active and expansive as they seek out new experiences.

• Eight-year-olds talk constantly and love to gossip.

Self-Concept and Independence

• Eight-year-olds have a greater awareness of self; they are less sensitive, less introspective, and less apt to withdraw. They are becoming individuals who are aware of themselves in the social world.

• They are able to judge and appraise themselves and are conscious of the ways in which they differ from other people.

• Eight-year-olds are concerned about how other people feel about them, and they can be demanding in their efforts to get information about themselves.

• They can work independently, but need direction.

Relating to Other Children and Adults

• Eight-year-olds are mature in their social relationships with others. Relationships with friends are positive. Friendships are closer and very important.

• There is a noticeable separation between boys and girls and both play at games that tend to exclude the opposite sex.

- They are usually friendly and cooperative, preferring mature jobs that resemble adult-like activities.
- They are more polite with strangers than they are at home and are able to hold their own in conversations with adults.

Games and Activities
- Eight-year-olds dislike playing alone. They prefer to be with an adult or another child. Action becomes the focus of all their play.
- Both boys and girls like cooking and baking and show an interest in foreign places and children from different times.
- The collections they began at seven now become more organized and classified.
- They tend to make up their own rules for games and they may even invent new games.
- Eight-year-olds like dramatic play, especially where they take the role of characters they have read about, seen, or heard about.
- Table games such as cards, parchesi, checkers, and dominoes are very popular.

When working with eight-year-olds, adults must remember that they are very social and like to be with peers. They gossip and talk constantly, passing notes from one to the other. This often gets out-of-hand when they are in group situations. In addition to their tendency to judge others, eight-year-olds are increasingly self-critical. For example, many children who liked artwork at six or seven may give it up at eight because they see the difference between the quality of their drawings and those of a friend.

In Summary
Children are individuals with their own special temperaments and idiosyncracies. The ages and stages children go through can vary tremendously from one child to the next and, by respecting the variousness of children, parents and other caregivers can help them develop strong and healthy self-concepts.

II - MIDDLE YEARS: AGES 9-11

The ages six to twelve are commonly known as the middle years of childhood. This is the time when children are in full bloom; they are no longer babies but the demands of adult life are still far away. All through this period children continue to develop their special personalities. They are getting to know more about themselves and the world in which they live and their slow steady growth can be observed. They grow in independence and become more able to take care of themselves. They also are eager adventurers who learn from their explorations but who often find, to their dismay and to the dismay of the adults around them, that they still have a lot to learn.

Each child is different and there are no set rules for rearing or teaching children. How children grow depends on the characteristics they inherit from their parents and, to a good extent, it depends on the guidance provided by parents and other adults. It also depends on the experiences youngsters have inside and outside of their homes.

Although each child's temperament makes her special, certain guidelines of child growth apply to most youngsters, and parents and other caregivers may find these guidelines helpful when working with the middle-years child.

- **In physical development,** height and weight increase slowly and evenly. Children gain about two or three inches in height each year. Body proportions also change. In contrast to the chunky body of the preschooler, during the middle years the trunk becomes slimmer, the chest becomes broader, and the arms and legs thin out.
- **In psychological development,** middle-years children can find themselves in conflict between the need to grow up and the

desire to remain a child forever. They want to grow up so that they can enjoy the prerogatives of adult life, but they also want to hold on to all the privileges of childhood.

During the middle years, boys and girls gradually become aware of sexual differences. Fortunately, children now are encouraged to try activities traditionally reserved for the opposite sex-a trend that is helping to break down sex-role stereotypes.

- **In social development,** the middle-years child may appear to be a staid traditionalist who accepts the authority of the family. The family is the main base of security and identity, although around the age of eleven the child begins to place more and more value on the peer group.

Ages and Stages

The information presented here about the ages and stages of children is only a *guide*. Physically, emotionally, and intellectually, each child grows and develops at his own rate. Some youngsters may be early bloomers. That is, they may have reached a stage of emotional or physical development beyond their chronological years. Understanding the characteristics of an age can be helpful to adults who work with or care for children. But, if adults are to foster optimal growth and development in children, they also must remain sensitive and responsive to children as individuals.

Nine-Year-Olds
General
Nine is a developmental middle zone.

- The nine-year-old shows a new maturity, self-confidence, and independence from adults.
- There is an increase in maturity and refinement of behavior. Judgmental tendencies are more discerning and objective. Nine-year-olds can evaluate themselves, find that they are lacking, but not feel guilty about it.

Self-Concept and Independence
- Nine-year-olds tend to be inner-directed and self-motivated.
- They have occasions of intense emotion and impatience, but their outbursts are less frequent and they show greater self-control. The inner-directed quality of their behavior allows nine-year-olds to become intently involved in activities.
- If forced to interrupt an activity, nine-year-olds will usually come back to it on their own.
- They can think and reason for themselves.
- They can be trusted.
- They may withdraw from surroundings to get a sense of self. They do not, however, retreat as much as they did when they were seven.
- Nine-year-olds do not feel impelled to boast and attack to protect themselves.

Relating to Other Children and Adults
- In their relationships with both adults and peers, they show consideration and fairness beyond that shown at a younger age.
- They can accept their own failures and mistakes, and they are willing to take responsibility for their own actions.
- Nine-year-olds have an increased awareness of sex and sex-differentiated behaviors.
- Girls can become concerned about their clothing and appearance. They take more interest in the "right" fashion.
- Friendships tend to be more solid, but occasionally nine-year-olds can have an intense dislike of the opposite sex, preferring to be with children of their own age and sex. Boys and girls both may begin to form clubs around various activities.
- Although their independence can be trying at times, they are often easier to work with than younger children who make great demands on adults.
- They are anxious to please and love to be chosen.

- Most of the mother-child conflict of the eight-year-old has disappeared, and the nine-year-old makes fewer demands on parents.
- Nine-year-olds usually have no problems with young children or older brothers and sisters. In fact, they can be very loyal to siblings.

Games and Activities
- Nine-year-olds spend much time in solitary activities of their own choosing.
- Bicycling, roller and ice skating, and swimming are physical activities they enjoy.
- They continue to enjoy the advanced table games they learned at eight.
- Materials and information attract the nine-year-old. Organized games or activities such as baseball, football, and basketball are popular. Many children at this age also have mastered basic reading and arithmetic and can use these skills to gain information, to solve problems, and to participate in games and recreation.

Ten-Year-Olds

General
Ten is the high point of childhood. Ten-year-olds have worked through the difficulties of home, school, and community. They now can take pride in their ability to fit in at home, at school, and at play with their peers. On occasion, there can be outbursts of anger, depression, or sadness, but these moods are short-lived and soon forgotten.
- Girls are slightly more advanced sexually than boys and already there is some evidence of the rapid sprint to maturity that will make them taller and heavier than boys their own age in a couple of years. Their bodies are rounding out and the softening of contours may begin. Some girls may even experience the first stages of breast development. Girls become concerned about their bodies and menstruation and about sexual activity in general.
- For boys physical changes are less marked, thus concern for the body and physical maturity is much less noticeable.

Self-Concept and Independence
- Ten-year-olds accept themselves as they are without worrying too much about their strengths and weaknesses. They are much less interested in evaluating themselves. They like their bodies and like what they can do both athletically and academically. Their self-acceptance is heightened by the acceptance accorded them by peers, families, and school.

Relating to Other Children and Adults
- Ten-year-olds like and enjoy their friends. Boys may move into loosely organized groups. Within these groups, boys may have particular friends, but there is a lot of switching around. Girls usually move in smaller groups and are likely to form more intense friendships and have more serious "falling outs" with their friends being "mad" and "not playing" or "not speaking" to one another as a result. There are times when ten-year-olds may seem to value their peer group more than their families.
- Teachers and other adults who interact with this age group are popular if they are fair and not partial to particular children in the group. Adults working with ten-year-olds need to be firm but not strict. At this age children like adult leaders to schedule activities and like to keep to the schedule.

Games and Activities
- They like outings and trips.
- They like organized games and belonging to clubs and groups.
- When working on a project they may need to get up and move about.

Eleven-Year-Olds

General
At this age, there is an accelerated growth pace.
- The eleven-year-old's activity level increases; energy and appetite also increase.
- There is a tendency at this age to forget manners, to be loud, rude, and boorish, and to take unnecessary chances as a means of defying adult authority. Riding bicycles in heavy traffic is an example of this kind of behavior.
- Eleven-year-olds quarrel a good deal with adults and lack emotional control although they can be cooperative and friendly with strangers. They need firmness and understanding from adults.

Self-Concept and Independence
- They can be belligerent because of their high energy level, which pushes them toward activities, but which sometimes leads to carelessness.
- The eleven-year-old is looking for new self-definition.
- They will often confront others with criticism in an effort to get attention. They can, however, admit faults.
- They will sometimes differ with parents on careers and have dreams of being famous while their parents try to temper such fantasies.
- An eleven-year-old, on occasion, will challenge parents and other adults on child-rearing practices.

Relating to Other Children and Adults
- Boys and girls have best friends and a group of other friends who are selected because of common interests and temperaments.
- Both boys and girls admit to being interested in the opposite sex and show their interest by teasing, joking, and showing off.
- Eleven-year-olds like to quarrel with others, but don't like others to argue with them.
- They can be cooperative, friendly, and pleasant with adults, but they need to be treated with understanding and firmness.
- Eleven-year-olds can feel left out from their peer group.

Games and Activities
- They don't like to work with materials that are complex, but they do like things that show off their rote skills.
- Eleven-year-olds have trouble understanding relationships and the complex combinations of events.

In Summary

Children are individuals with their own special temperaments and idiosyncracies. The ages and stages children go through can vary tremendously from one child to the next and, by respecting the variousness of children, parents and other caregivers can help them develop strong and healthy self-concepts.

III - ADOLESCENTS

> *The young are prone to desire and in regard to sexual desire they exercise no self-restraint. They are changeful, too, and fickle in their desires. They are passionate, irascible, and apt to be carried away by their impulses. They are slaves, too, of their passion.*

A distinguished scientist and philosopher made this observation over 2000 years ago. To some, Aristotle's lament might suggest that adolescents haven't changed much since the days of ancient Athens, but recent research indicates that what hasn't changed is adults' *perceptions* of adolescents. Surveys of adolescents and their parents show that their values and attitudes are generally quite compatible. The famous "generation gap" appears to be an invention of the news media in response to a small but highly visible group of adolescents whose challenge to the older generation in the 1960s was mistakenly interpreted as representative.

What is it about the stage of life between childhood and adulthood that makes it so difficult for adults to understand? Although adolescence is not equally troublesome in all societies and for all families, adults' reports of its stressful nature are sufficiently widespread to warrant attention.

Change-physical, mental, and social change-is the most notable quality of adolescence and accounts for a good deal of the difficulty.

Physical Changes

The most obvious physical change during adolescence is rapid acceleration of growth. Within two years before or after age 12 for girls and age 14 for boys, a growth spurt occurs. The rate of gain in height and weight typically doubles for a year or more. Physical growth takes place in a fairly consistent sequence, beginning at the extremities and moving inward. Head, hands, and feet enlarge first, followed by arms and legs, then trunk. The broadening of male shoulders and female hips that characterizes adult body form occurs last. Overall growth is accompanied, though not always in the same order or at the same rate, by maturation of the reproductive organs and glands and by the appearance of pubic and underarm hair, and facial hair in males.

Together, these physical changes accomplish the biological aspect of adolescence, which is known as pubescence: they transform a child into an adult, one who is able to have children.

But this physical transformation is not as simple for the person going through it as it sounds when described in the abstract. For one thing, the ages at which pubescence begins and is completed vary as much as four years among different young people. Furthermore, the period from beginning to completion may be as little as 18 months for some and as much as six years for others. As a result of this variation, any group of early adolescents is likely to include young people who are at very different points in pubescence. Because girls enter pubescence, on the average, two years earlier than boys, the greatest variation among girls' physical maturation occurs during ages 11-13, while in boys it is during ages 13-15.

Rapid change combined with wide variation among individuals tend to make adolescents extremely sensitive to their appearance. At no other time in life are feelings about the self (self-esteem) so closely tied to feelings about the body (body image). Physical appearance also affects the ways in which other people treat an adolescent. Adults tend to expect adult behavior from a 15-year-old boy who is six feet tall and shaves regularly, but they will readily excuse childish behavior on the part of his classmate who, though the same age, has not yet begun his growth spurt. Perhaps even more importantly, peers judge one another on the basis of physical size and appearance. Early maturation can be an advantage for boys but often is not for girls because it puts them out-of-step with their peers.

The physical changes of pubescence, therefore, have direct effects on adolescents' social relations. They also affect emotions. The maturation of the gonads reproductive glandschanges the balance of hormones in the body, which can result in new sensitivities to the environment. For example, an adolescent may have a heightened sensitivity to loss of sleep, which results in moodiness or outbursts of temper. Cyclical changes in hormonal balance, especially among girls but also to some extent among boys, are associated with changes in emotions, behavior, and thinking. Since these cycles are new to adolescents, they may not be handled well.

Mental Changes

The most important mental change during adolescence is the growth in capacity for abstract thinking. Before age 11 or 12, children think in terms of concrete objects and groups of objects. Their reasoning is simple and direct. It does not allow for much complexity or subtlety. Given a problem to solve, the child tends to plunge into it with first one possible solution and then another until she either finds the correct solution or gives up. Confronted with a moral dilemma, she responds on the basis of a rule, which may or may not be appropriately applied.

By age 16, most adolescents have transcended this simple way of thinking, though not all of them adopt the most complex forms of reasoning. Nor do all use the same types of reasoning about all issues, any more than adults do. Adolescents begin to achieve the capacity to approach a problem systematically. Instead of moving immediately into the trying out of an assortment of solutions, they can analyze the problem and arrive at some tentative conclusions about what sorts of solutions probably will and will not work. Then they can proceed in a logical fashion to test and evaluate solutions, gaining a greater understanding of the problem along the way.

Moral issues become much more complex than they are for young children because adolescents are able to understand that two sound rules or principles might conflict in some cases. For example, they will understand that in certain situations, the values of friendship and honesty conflict, and they will struggle with a question about whether someone should report a friend for breaking a rule. Younger children are more likely to choose either one principle or the other without recognizing the dilemma. Furthermore, adolescents outgrow the childish belief that only evil people do bad things. They understand accident and circumstances involve even the best-intentioned people in undesirable actions. They are, therefore, likely to be more understanding and forgiving of human frailty than young children, though their interest in principles can also make adolescents morally rigid at times.

Along with the capacity to think abstractly comes the realization that what exists is only one of many possibilities. Thinking about those possibilities becomes a fascinating activity. The real is frequently compared to the ideal and found wanting. Because they can conceive of a more ideal worJd without having to bother themselves with all the details of how it might be achieved and what drawbacks it might have, adolescents are often impatient with the real world and with the failure of adults to have made it better already.

This capacity to think about many possible realities is important, given the momentous choices adolescents will make as they move into adulthood and choose career directions, educational paths, and mates. Without it they are likely to drift into the first opportunities that arise without considering what the other possibilities might be, which are most desirable, and which are feasible.

Similarly, the ability to reason about moral issues is necessary if a person is to establish a personal moral code. Rules and principles simply accepted from parents and other authorities are essential to children, but adolescents need to think through rules and principles and consider the alternatives in order to adopt or adapt them for themselves. An adolescent who does not go through the process of questioning principles and values may be without guidance when confronted with a new and complex moral dilemma or when one or another of his/her basic principles is seriously challenged.

Social Changes

Because of their physical and mental growth, adolescents are no longer treated like children. The expectations adults and peers have of them change and their behavior changes. Thus the social world in which they live changes in important ways.

One of the most obvious social changes is the initiation of serious interest in and interactions with young people of the opposite sex. The physical and emotional changes of pubescence described above lead to strong new feelings between girls and boys. Even before they begin to act upon these feelings by dating and engaging in other heterosexual activities, many adolescents begin to have "crushes" on opposite-sex peers, and sometimes on same-sex peers and on adults. These one-way emotional attachments simply indicate the presence of new emotional capacities, but they can be difficult for the adolescent to understand and deal with. Learning to handle the emotions and behavior that go along with attracting and forming emotional attachments to members of the opposite sex can be stressful, in addition to being terribly exciting.

The social world of the adolescent changes in other ways as well. A sixteen-year-old may notice that adults are treating her more like one of them, engaging in real conversation, for example, instead of saying "My, how you've grown," and asking about school. She may also notice that she enjoys this adult conversation when just a year or two before she would have preferred to go out and play.

By the age of sixteen, adolescents are being given many privileges formerly reserved for adults. In most places they can drive a car, quit school, and hold a job. Although it is usually against the law, they can fairly easily smoke and drink alcoholic beverages.

Relations with parents change too. As they grow more mature, adolescents are less dependent on their parents than they were earlier. They might be able to live on their own. They have ideas of their own and are reconsidering some of the beliefs and values their parents have taught them. They receive emotional support from peers. Sometimes their peers' values are inconsistent with their parents'. For all these reasons, they become less deferent to their parents' wishes and opinions, adopting a more independent and often a more aggressive stance.

Modern industrial societies demand highly educated workers and do not need the labor of children. Therefore, most young people experience a long gap between the attainment of physical adulthood and adult status. Marriage, parenthood, and full-time paid employment are the principal indicators of adult status in our society. At least two ambiguities arise from this social definition of adulthood. One is that young people are expected to postpone marriage and to remain economically dependent on their parents for several years after they are physically capable of reproduction and full-time employment. A second is that while many young people "prolong their adolescence" by enrolling in college and then in graduate or professional school, many of their peers are entering full-time employment, getting married, and starting families. Although adolescence can be an enjoyable stage of life because of the freedom from adult obligations, it can also be a frustrating time because adult privileges are withheld.

Difficulties for Parents

Adolescents are no longer children; they and their parents have to work out new ways of dealing with each other that recognize their growing but not yet complete maturity. Parents must realize that they can no longer control their offspring in many important areas. Adolescents simply have too many opportunities to do as they please. Young people, who are often adamant in demanding relief from parental control, need to understand that freedom demands responsibility. They cannot expect their parents to give them adult privileges regarding their social activities and then excuse them from household obligations because they are only children.

One of the reasons adolescents often seem to be a burden to their parents is that parents have to change the way they treat their adolescents. Parental behavior that has developed over several years and has been rather effective becomes obsolete. New behavior, a new parental style, is called for.

Being required to deal with new challenges and to behave in different ways is always difficult, but it can be especially difficult for parents of adolescents who are simultaneously experiencing stress in other parts of their lives. The term "midlife crisis" has become popular in recent years in recognition that many people go through a period of self-examination and often of serious readjustment in middle age as they realize they have relatively few years left to accomplish what they aspire to. Two life cycle changes in the family are associated with this midlife crisis: one is the death of one's own parents and the other is the maturation of one's children. People at this point frequently have to accept the fact that they will not achieve the prominence in their careers that they might have wanted. Common responses to this "crisis" include career and marital changes.

Parents who are experiencing crises of this magnitude are likely to feel overwhelmed by the challenges of dealing with their rapidly changing adolescents. But even parents who feel satisfied and secure in most aspects of their lives may have difficulty coping with their adolescent children.

What Adults Can Do for Adolescents

There are times when the adolescent says, "Why don't you just leave me alone!" and the adult wants to say, "Alright, I will." That is not a solution, however, because adolescents need adults to help them achieve adulthood themselves. The following suggestions may prove helpful to adults who work with adolescents, but they cannot be treated as a cookbook. Just as adolescents refuse to follow many adult "recipes" for proper behavior because they need to work out their own behavioral code, adults must be flexible and resourceful in responding to adolescents. There is no single way to do it.

1. Be honest. With their newly developed capacity for abstract thinking, adolescents become fascinated with principles and with consistency. They are severe critics of adults they think are hypocritical or two-faced. Most adolescents are sophisticated enough to see through dishonesty or pretention in adults who are close to them. They tend to be skeptical at what adults tell them and to welcome any confirmation of that skepticism.

2. Be open. Adolescents want and need to talk about things with their parents and other adults close to them. But they also need to maintain their privacy and their independence. Therefore, adult-adolescent conversations cannot be one-sided, with the adolescent baring his soul and the adult listening and offering advice. Adolescents need to know that some of the same concerns they struggle with are concerns of adults too.

Sexuality is one of the most insistent concerns of adolescents because it is a new one, brought out by their sexual maturation. Adults cannot be very helpful to adolescents about sexual issues unless they, as adults, are comfortable with their own sexuality. They must be willing to acknowledge the complexity of the issues and the strength of the social and emotional pressures. In our society the "official" morality is that sexual relations are limited to marriage, yet television, movies, magazines, songs on the radio, and even billboards bombard us constantly with the message that sexual attractiveness is the most important personal quality and that unrestrained sexual behavior is good. Like adolescents, adults can find this contradiction confusing, and they should be willing to discuss it.

3. Set clear and consistent limits. Most children will abide by rules their parents or other adults set down just because they are rules, at least as long as the adult is looking. Adolescents are much more likely to want to know why a particular rule or expectation has been stated. Adults should respect this need for explanation and should allow for some negotiation regarding rules for behavior. But, consistent with the recommendation to be honest, adults should not hesitate to say what they believe is absolutely essential and is not open to negotiation.

There may be some rules or limits set by parents that adolescents continue to violate because they are independent enough to do so. Parents may have to acknowledge that they cannot control what the adolescent does away from home but make clear that they will not allow it in the home and then follow through with that prohibition.

4. Remember that growing up means becoming independent. Effective parents, and other adults who succeed in helping adolescents become adults, are able to accept young people making choices that they would not have made and behaving in ways they do not approve of. That is what independence means. Young adults who still do as they are told all the time are immature and unprepared to face a world in which they are constantly required to decide for themselves. Most adolescents become adults who are a source of pride and happiness for their parents and for the other adults who worked with them. But for this to happen, they must first establish some independence, and that can require a painful break.

Adolescents undergo dramatic physical and mental changes in a short period of time, and they are given a confusing in-between place in our society. The period can be painful for the adolescents and for the adults who are close to them. But it is a necessary process both for the adolescents to come of age and for our society to renew itself through the questions, the new perspective, and the new talents that each group of young people brings into adulthood.